HUNANIAETH GYMREIG
WELSH IDENTITY

ch 20

Hunaniaeth Gymreig

Welsh Identity

Golygydd/Editor

T. Graham Williams, B.A.

Grŵp Ysgrifennu Rhiwfawr Writers' Group
2004

Argraffiad cyntaf – Mai 2004
Ailargraffiad – Mehefin 2004

Argraffwyd yng Nghymru gan Wasg Dinefwr, Llandybïe

ISBN 0-9547278-0-0

First impression – May 2004
Reprinted – June 2004

Designed and published by
© Rhiwfawr Writers' Group, 2004

Dyluniwyd y clawr
gan
Rory Clark
Designed the front cover

Printed in Wales by Dinefwr Press, Llandybïe

Cynnwys/Contents

Rhagair

AR ÔL GWNEUD SAWL cais i berswadio'r Brifysgol Agored i gyflwyno cwrs ar Gymru a'i phobl fel rhan annatod, ond opsiynol, o gwrs gradd, rhoddwyd caniatâd inni, ymhen hir a hwyr, yn 1982, i ddatblygu ac i ysgrifennu cwrs gradd anrhydedd: *Wales: A Study of Cultural and National Identity*, cyn belled ag y byddai'r gwaith wedi'i anelu at astudiaeth lefel pedwar (anrhydedd arbennig). Cwrs ydoedd a ymgorfforai ddulliau technegau dysgu hirbell – testunau darllen, aseiniadau ysgrifenedig manwl, ynghyd â chefnogaeth dosbarthiadau tiwtorial a gynhelid ar ffurf cynadledda dros y ffôn a chyfres o ysgolion undydd rhanbarthol. Neilltuwyd y cwrs ar gyfer myfyrwyr â chanddynt gefndir academaidd a safonau priodol ac a fyddai'n barod i ddangos ymroddiad cadarn i'r cwrs. Seiliwyd themâu'r cwrs ar lenyddiaeth ymchwil sylweddol, yn enwedig daearyddiaeth ddynol, hanes cymdeithasol a gwleidyddol ac astudiaethau cymunedol. Disgwylid i fyfyrwyr nid yn unig ymdopi ag ystod eang o syniadau heriol ond hefyd i ddwyn i'w hastudiaethau wybodaeth a dealltwriaeth wedi'u tynnu o'u profiadau a'u cefndir teuluol eu hunain. Yn naturiol, ar y cychwyn, yr oeddem wedi meddwl y byddai'r mwyafrif o'r myfyrwyr yn byw yng Nghymru neu o leiaf y byddai ganddynt gysylltiadau Cymreig cryf. Ond yn ystod pedair blynedd y cwrs, canfuom fod ein myfyrwyr yn byw yn Lloegr a'r Alban, yn ogystal ag yng Nghymru. Mewn gwirionedd, mewn un flwyddyn, trigai'r myfyriwr a enillodd farciau uchaf anrhydedd dosbarth cyntaf yng Ngogledd yr Alban, lle y gweithiai mewn distyllfa whisgi, ond nid oedd ganddo gysylltiad uniongyrchol â Chymru na'i phobl! Adlewyrchir yr holl brif themâu a archwiliasom yng nghasgliad y papurau allweddol, *The Welsh and Their Country: Selected Readings in the Social Sciences*, a olygwyd gan Ian Hume a W. T. R. Pryce, ac a gyhoeddwyd gan Wasg Gomer, Landysul, yn 1986 – ond sydd erbyn hyn allan o brint.

Yn ystod y cyfnod hwn, yr oedd y ddau ohonom yn ymwneud hefyd â chyrsiau eraill y Brifysgol Agored; ac, yn ychwanegol at hyn, yr oedd arnom y cyfrifoldeb o benodi ac arolygu pob tiwtor yng Nghymru a gynhaliai gyrsiau niferus a oedd yn rhan annatod o ddarpariaeth y Brifysgol Agored ar gyfer y Gyfadran Gwyddorau Cymdeithasol. Canfuom fod y gwaith o ddatblygu'r cwrs newydd yn ddiddorol tu hwnt a hynny er gwaethaf y pwysau trwm ar ein hamser personol. Yn ychwanegol yr oedd pob myfyriwr, ym mhob blwyddyn, yn rhai o'r bobl fwyaf gweithgar ac ymroddedig y cawsom y fraint o gydweithio â hwy erioed.

Nodweddion unigryw hunaniaeth genedlaethol a diwylliannol Cymru, ein gwlad ni, fel y'u hadlewyrchir mewn termau gwyddonol ac ysgolheigaidd, oedd sylwedd ein prif themâu – themâu a ymddengys a fu'n allweddol i ysgogi ein myfyrwyr ac felly yn gweithredu fel dull o fynegi dealltwriaeth. Prif ysgogydd y llyfr newydd hwn, a elwir, yn briodol iawn, *Hunaniaeth Gymreig: Welsh Identity*, yw ei gasglwr a'i olygydd, Mr. T. Graham Williams (a adwaenir hefyd yn ôl ei enw barddol 'Cefnfab') ef oedd yn un o'n myfyrwyr arloesol ac yr oedd ei frwdfrydedd yn heintus. Y mae'n amlwg, a hynny oherwydd natur yr ysgrifau yn y casgliad hwn, fod y brwdfrydedd hwnnw wedi parhau! Yn ystod ei amser gyda ni, a thra'n ymdopi'n arbennig gyda phynciau penodol yn ymwneud â hunaniaeth Gymreig a godai yn ein cwrs, dadleuai Mr. Williams, gydag argyhoeddiad, y dylid ystyried rôl profiad bywyd yr unigolyn ynghyd â'i deimladau personol er mwyn gwir ddeall ac i roi amlygiad i'r hyn yw 'Cymreictod'. Ond oherwydd cyfyngiadau amser nid oeddem yn medru archwilio'n llawn yr agweddau pwysig hyn. Felly, croesawn y llyfr newydd hwn gyda'i gyfraniadau ffres ysgogol, yr adfyfrdodau personol a'r mynegi barn ynglŷn â beth y mae'n ei olygu i fod yn Gymro neu'n Gymraes. Dyma'r tro cyntaf i'r gweithiau hyn gael eu cyhoeddi.

Gan mai tynnu ar hanes bucheddau a phrofiadau personol a wneir, fe ellir ystyried y cyfraniadau newydd hyn yn bennaf, efallai, fel rhai archwiliol eu natur. Er enghraifft, y mae Maggie Wagstaff ac Annette Thomas yn rhannu gyda ni eu gwerthfawrogiad o 'fro' draddodiadol y teulu tra dywed Jean Williams mai carwriaeth a ddaeth â theimlad dwfn o Gymreictod iddi. Y mae Mr. T. Graham Williams (Cefnfab) yn cofio am yr argraff gynnes gyntaf a wnaeth Dr. Gwynfor Evans arno pan oedd yn arweinydd ysbrydoledig Plaid Cymru. Diau fod y gwron hwnnw wedi gwerthfawrogi'n fawr ddawn ddihafal Graham i ddehongli gweithiau Dylan Thomas. Mewn ysgrif arall, dywed Graham wrthym beth oedd yr Urdd yn ei olygu ac yn dal ei olygu iddo. Fel a geir yn fynych yng Nghymru, lle y rhannwn enwau cyffelyb, ceir cyfraniadau gan ddau 'Brian' Davies. Y mae'r naill wedi ysgrifennu ar 'The Welsh Gentry, 1750-1850'; a'r llall yn rhoi i ni olwg ar y modd y mae dyn o'r cymoedd yn gweld Cymreictod ('Welsh Identity without Illusion'). Mae 'Bryan' Davies, wedyn, yn edrych ar gerddoriaeth fel ffordd o fynegi hunaniaeth ('Picking up the Pieces'). Y mae 'Leon' yn 'A Shot in the Dark' yn sôn am sefyllfaoedd gwaith traddodiadol yn yr hen Gymru ddiwydiannol, ac adleisiau o Gymreictod yn y Dwyrain Canol, 'The Great Escape', gan Marjorie Showalla. Tynnu ar brofiadau o ymgartrefu yng Nghymru a wna Roger Whatcott yn 'Identity' a sôn am ailddarganfod personol a wna J. Beynon Phillips yn 'Y Gymraes Newydd'. Â Euros Jones Evans yn ôl i gyfnod ei lencyndod gan olrhain rhai o'r profiadau hynny a fowldiodd y 'Cymro' o'i fewn. Yn 'Beth yw'r Ots?' y mae Dylan Iorwerth trwy gyfrwng holi ac ateb miniog yn peri inni ystyried beth yw gwir Gymreictod.

Y mae'r casgliad hwn o ysgrifau yn llawn syniadau a phrofiadau cyfoethog a fydd yn sicr o ysgogi'r darllenwyr nid yn unig i adfyfyrio a meddwl yn ddwys am eu gwreiddiau a chyfnodau'r gorffennol ond hefyd am y wlad heddiw yr ydym yn byw ynddi.

IAN HUME
DR. W. T. R. PRYCE

Ar un adeg Aelodau o Gyfadran y Gwyddor Cymdeithasol,
Y Brifysgol Agored yng Nghymru,
Caerdydd.

Foreword

AFTER SEVERAL ATTEMPTS to persuade the Open University to present a course on Wales and its people as an integral, but optional, part of undergraduate studies, eventually, in 1982, we were permitted to develop and write the new honours-level course *Wales: A Study of Cultural and National Identity,* provided that the work was pitched at the fourth (specialist honours) level of study. The course was designed using distance-teaching techniques – printed texts, in-depth written assignments, with supportive tutorials using a conference telephone network and a few regional day schools. Admission was restricted to students who, with the appropriate academic background and achieved standards, could demonstrate strong commitment. The course themes drew on a substantial research literature, especially in human geography, social and political history and major community studies. Students were expected to cope with a wide range of challenging ideas but also to bring to their studies knowledge and understanding drawn from personal life experience and family background. Naturally, at first we had assumed that the great majority of students would be resident in Wales or at least would have strong Welsh connections. But during the four years of presentation, we found that our students lived in England and Scotland, as well as in Wales itself. In fact, in one year, the student earning the highest overall first-class honours marks was living in northern Scotland, where he worked in a whisky distillery, but he had no direct connection whatsoever with Wales or its people! All the major themes that we explored are reflected in our collection of key papers, *The Welsh and Their Country: Selected Readings in the Social Sciences,* edited by Ian Hume and W. T. R. Pryce, published by the Gomer Press, Llandysul, in 1986 – now long out of print.

At this time, both of us were also much involved in other courses at the Open University; and, in addition, we carried heavy responsibilities for the appointment and supervision of all the tutors in Wales for the numerous courses integral to the Open University's offerings in the Faculty of Social Sciences. We found the developmental work on our new course totally engaging, despite severe pressures on our personal time. Moreover, the students, every one, in every year of presentation, were some of the most dedicated, hard working and committed people with whom we have ever worked.

The distinctive cultural and national identity of Wales, our own country, as reflected in scientific and scholarly terms, constituted our major themes – themes that seem to have been instrumental in switching on our students and thus functioning as an enabler for the articulation of understanding. The prime moving force behind this new book, entitled, appropriately, *Hunaniaeth Gymreig: Welsh Identity*, its compiler and editor, Mr. T. Graham Williams (then and now also known by his bardic name 'Cefnfab'), was amongst the first set of pioneering students. His enthusiasm was infectious. Evidently, from the nature of the essays included in this collection, it continues unabated! During his time with us, Mr. Williams, whilst coping very fully with the specific nature of the Welsh identity issues as raised in our course, also argued, very cogently, for the role of life experience and personal insight in understanding and articulating 'Welshness'. But with severe time constraints we were not able to fully explore these important aspects. So today, we welcome this new book, with its fresh stimulating contributions, reflections and articulations on what it means to be Welsh, all of which appear in print for the first time.

Drawn from personal life histories or specific experiences, in many respects each of these new contributions can be regarded at this stage, perhaps, as primarily explorative in nature. Here, for example, Maggie Wagstaff and Annette Thomas share with us their appreciation of a family's traditional 'bro', whilst for Jean Williams it was a love affair that brought a deep sense of Welshness. Mr. T. Graham Williams (Cefnfab) recounts his first warm impressions of Dr. Gwynfor Evans, then the inspiring leader of Plaid Cymru, who clearly must have greatly appreciated Graham's lively interpretations of the works of Dylan Thomas; and later, in a separate contribution, Graham tells us what the 'Urdd' means and has meant for him. Typical of many situations in Wales, where we all share a relatively small number of names, there are two 'Brian' Davieses and a third 'Bryan' Davies – writing, respectively, on 'The Welsh Gentry, 1750-1850'; on how a valleys-man perceives Welshness ('Welsh Identity without Illusion'); and on music as an expression of identity ('Picking up the Pieces'). Other contributions bring home traditional work situations in old industrial Wales ('A Shot in the Dark' by Leon); echoes of Welshness in the Middle East (The Great Escape by Marjorie Showalla), or draw on the experience of settling in Wales or personal rediscovery ('Identity' by Roger Whatcott, 'Y Gymraes Newydd' by J. Beynon Phillips, 'Very Welsh' by Euros Jones Evans), or, as in Dylan Iorwerth's splendid 'Beth yw'r Ots?', provide sharp tools for our own use in realising who we are or who we are becoming.

This is a collection of writings rich in ideas, experience and meaning that will stimulate much personal reflection and deep thoughts on origins, on times past and on the country today in which we live.

IAN HUME
DR. W. T. R PRYCE

Sometime Members of the Faculty of Social Sciences,
The Open University in Wales,
Cardiff.

Cyflwyniad

ARDDIAD Y LLYFR hwn oedd ffrwyth y profiad o ddilyn cwrs gan y Brifysgol Agored, sef *"D423: Wales – a study of cultural and national identity"*, a ysgrifennwyd gan Ian Hume a Dr W. T. R. Pryce.

Datgelodd y cwrs wahanol agweddau o'r bywyd Cymreig; yn hanesyddol, gwleidyddol, diwylliannol, ac yr oedd yn ddiddorol a thrylwyr. Yr unig beth yn absennol oedd storïau, erthyglau neu farddoniaeth a fyddai wedi ychwanegu mwy o awyrgylch at y cynnwys. Penderfynwyd, felly, cael sylwadau nifer o awduron am *hanfod* y bywyd Cymreig. Cnewyllyn yr awduron hyn oedd Grŵp Ysgrifennu Rhiwfawr. Er mwyn cyfoethogi'r fenter ymhellach, fe roddwyd gwahoddiad i rai o bobl adnabyddus y wlad i gynnig eu barn hwy o beth yw 'Hunaniaeth Gymreig'. Mae'r cyfraniadau hyn, yn ôl y disgwyl, yn ddwyieithog.

T. GRAHAM WILLIAMS, B.A.
Rhiwfawr, 2004

Introduction

THE SOURCE of this book was the experience gained through perusing an Open University course, namely *"D423: Wales – a study of cultural and national identity"*, written and devised by Ian Hume and Dr. W. T. R. Pryce.

This course revealed various aspects of Welsh life; its historical, political and cultural background, which was both interesting and thorough. Only stories, articles and poetry were absent, which would have added more atmosphere to the given content. Therefore, it was decided to obtain the views of several authors as to what is the *essence* of a Welsh way of life. The nucleus of these authors was the Rhiwfawr Writer's Group. In order to enrich the project further, some of the country's foremost authors were invited to express their opinion as to what is a 'Welsh Identity'. It goes without saying that these contributions have been bilingually expressed.

T. GRAHAM WILLIAMS, B.A.
Rhiwfawr, 2004

Yr Awduron a'u Gwaith

MAE'R AWDURON a enwir gyntaf yn cynnwys Grŵp Ysgrifennu Rhiwfawr. Cyn löwr yw Leon sydd wedi sôn am ddigwyddiad yn y lofa . . . ac, yn ôl y disgwyl, mae yn hiwmor du. Trwy ei brofiad o symud o Portsmouth mae Roger Whatcott yn ysgrifennu am yr hyn mae hunaniaeth Gymreig yn ei olygu iddo ef. Un sydd dros bedwar ugain mlwydd oed yw Phyllis Wagstaff. Galw i gof ei dyddiau ysgol yn Derbyshire mae Phyllis, a fu yn fuddiol iddi maes o law pan fabwysiadodd y ffordd Gymreig o fyw. Cymharu ei bywyd cynnar yn Chesterfield â'r mwynhad a gafodd wedi iddi symud i Gymru a wna Maggie Wagstaff. Tra bod ei stori gyntaf yn Saesneg mae ei hail un yn gyfan gwbl yn y Gymraeg. Sôn am gynhesrwydd y Cymry mae Jean E. Williams, a sut bu hyn yn gefnogol iddi yn ystod argyfwng teuluol. Adrodd ei phrofiad fel metron mewn ysbyty yn y Dwyrain Canol mae Marjorie Showalla, a sut i'r gwrthdaro a fu yno oddi ar y chwedegau ymlaen ymyrryd ar ei theimladau Cymreig. Yn arwain i'r stori flaenorol mae erthygl gan Cefnfab sydd yn datgelu beth ddigwyddodd yng Ngheredigion yn ystod y bedwaredd ganrif ar bymtheg, a fu mor berthnasol i deimladau Marjorie pan ddihangodd am ei bywyd o Aden. Cyfranna Cefnfab erthyglau a barddoniaeth am Angueddfa Werin Sain Ffagan, Urdd Gobaith Cymru a chysylltiadau Dylan Thomas a Gwynfor Evans.

Gwahoddwyd nifer o awduron amlwg i gyfrannu i'r llyfr, gan gynnwys y bardd llwyddiannus, J. Beynon Phillips, sydd yn sôn am ddirywiad yr iaith Gymraeg. Bardd disglair arall yw Iwan Bryn Williams sydd yn cofio y diweddar Emrys Davies a chwaraeodd griced i Forgannwg. Mae rygbi yn cael sylw hefyd yn y llyfr trwy i'r Golygydd ymgomio â Clive Rowlands yn nhafodiaith Cwm Tawe. Galw i gof mae Clive sut y bu i ganu'r Cymry ei ysbrydoli. Diddorol yw nodi bod tri o'r awduron yn rhannu yr enw Brian Davies. Gŵr o Ystradgynlais yw un o ohonynt, sydd yn sôn am ymgais y sgweier-iaid Cymreig i efelychu eu cyffelyb yn Lloegr, tra bod Brian Davies, Curadur Amgueddfa Pontypridd, yn canolbwyntio ar gymhlethdod hunaniaeth y rhai sydd yn byw yn y cymoedd ac yn deillio o dras wahanol. Nid yw cerddoriaeth heb gael ei anghofio, chwaeth, am fod yna erthygl ddiddorol wedi cael ei hysgrifennu ar y testun gyda'r cysylltiadau Cymreig. Yr awdur yw Bryan Davies y cyfeil-ydd enwog o Ferndale. Mae Annette Thomas o Gapel Ucha' yn cofio ei thad-cu a fu'n bugeilio ar Fynydd yr Epynt. Cafwyd erthygl deilwng arall ar y thema ddyrys hon gan Euros Jones Evans. Cywydd coffa i Wmffra, yr hen ganwr eisteddfodol, yw cyfraniad cywrain Karen Owen. Ac i goroni'r cyfan cawn Dylan Iorwerth i fynegi ei farn yntau o ba beth yw 'hunaniaeth Gymreig'.

The Authors and their Works

THE FIRST MENTIONED authors comprise the Rhiwfawr Writers' Group. Leon is a former miner and has written a story about an incident at a colliery . . . and, as to be expected, it is black humour. Roger Whatcott has written about what 'Welsh identity' means to him, through his experience of moving from Portsmouth to Wales. Phyllis Wagstaff, our octogenarian writer, recalls her schooldays in Derbyshire and how they eventually proved to be beneficial in adapting to a Welsh way of life. Maggie Wagstaff compares her earlier life in Chesterfield with the one that she enjoys now in Wales. Her first story is in English whilst she has written the second one entirely in Welsh. Jean E. Williams writes about the warmth of the Welsh people that were so supportive to her during a domestic crisis. Marjorie Showalla relates her experience as a matron in the Middle East. She explains how she was continually caught up in the conflict that occurred there from the 1960's onwards and how her Welsh feelings caused a conflict within herself during this particular time. Preceding this story is an article written by Cefnfab about events that happened in Cardiganshire during the Nineteenth Century, which are similar to Marjorie's feelings whilst she was escaping from Aden. Cefnfab has also contributed poetry and articles in both English and Welsh about the Saint Fagan Folk Museum, Urdd Gobaith Cymru and Dylan Thomas' involvement with Gwynfor Evans.

The authors who have been invited to contribute to the book include J. Beynon Phillips, a highly successful poet, who writes about the demise of the Welsh language. Iwan Bryn Williams is another brilliant poet who relates what he remembers of the late Emrys Davies, who played cricket for Glamorgan. Rugby is also mentioned in the book through the Editor's conversation with Clive Rowlands in the Swansea Valley dialect. Clive recollects how

Welsh singing has always been so inspirational to him. It is interesting to note that three of the authors share the name Brian Davies.
One of them is an Ystradgynlais man who writes about how former
Welsh squires attempted to copy the lifestyle of their English counterparts, whilst Brian Davies, Curator of the Pontypridd Museum,
focuses on the complex identity of a valley's mixed origin. The
subject of music has not been forgotten, for there is a most infor-
mative and interesting article that examines the various sources of
Welsh music. This has been written by Bryan Davies of Ferndale,
the well-known accompanist. Annette Thomas of Upper Chapel
has written about her grandfather who was 'An Epynt Shepherd'.
Euros Jones Evans' article reveals another facet regarding this complex subject. There is a superb poem in the form of cynghanedd by
the established poet Karen Owen. It is a cywydd in memory of
Wmffra a very much loved eisteddfod singer. Dylan Iorwerth, winner
of the Crown at the Llanelli National Eisteddfod in the year 2000,
has also kindly contributed a fine piece of work on the Welsh identity.

Identity

by

ROGER WHATCOTT

WHAT IS "I den-ti-ti"? Look up the word in a dictionary and the definition you are given is: "The state of being identical, absolute sameness; one's individuality; absolute equality between two expressions; an equation expressing such equality". There is also an entry for old identity: "An old inhabitant". So, what informed meaning can we gain from all that? Mainly, I suppose, being individual, unlike any other person. In my youth I remember we had identity cards giving one's name and date of birth, which identified everyone as a unique person. So yes, one can agree that your individuality identifies you, so how would you describe an English or a Welsh identity? What is Englishness or Welshness? As I was born in England, presumably I have an English identity; but, I wonder, just how much that national identity tag really applies to me, and, if I had been born in Wales, would I have been any different?

Taking an impartial view of the subject, there is a question that I would like to pose. Is there really a fundamental difference between the people born in England and Wales? It is, after all, only the consequence of history – where our forefathers were born – that identifies our nationality. I realised this after I moved to Wales, and sensed that people here have had a very similar pattern of life as those who lived in Portsmouth, where I was born and spent most of my life.

My early years
After a World War II bomb inflicted major damage to my parents'

19

house – along with many thousands of others in Portsmouth – they moved to number 39, Hercules Street, a street like many others in the city. It had two long terraces of houses; our side of the street had pavements right up to the front door while on the other – "posh" – side, the houses had forecourts with wooden gates. All the residents seemed to live quite happily together, forming a little community with all the apparent lack of privacy that such a close-living environment entails.

People were always ready to help sort out others' problems and would freely offer their individual skills if they were needed. Amongst the working people in the street were a nurse, a policeman, a lay preacher, a court usher, a carpenter, a car mechanic, several dockyardsmen and even a bookie's runner. Some of them were real characters; there was one elderly woman who, although not known for the cleanliness of her own house, would readily go to the aid of a sick neighbour, scrubbing her house spotless, and preparing meals for the family. She was also the one called upon to "lay out" a body after death, ready for the undertakers.

These were working-class people, in some cases quite poor, but honest and generous with a great sense of pride in themselves and their homes. Front windows were cleaned at least once a week and, on a daily basis, doorsteps were scrubbed and brass door knockers, letterboxes and house number plates polished.

So, what led me to leave Portsmouth, with all its associations and happy memories which have certainly helped to shape my personality? What eventually led me to Wales?

A chance for change

An increasing disillusionment with city life chanced to coincide with an opportunity to take a redundancy/early retirement package from the Museums Service, when I was 51. After talking it over with my wife, I decided to take advantage of the option while the going was good; I realised that if I didn't, there would not be another chance. In time, my wife decided that she would like to take a break from teaching as well, so we began to consider plans for the future.

Having already enjoyed holidays in Wales, we had an idea of the different areas, the towns and the countryside. This influenced our decision to search for a new home here. We therefore began to look for a place that would afford us a more relaxed way of life, with perhaps a larger garden so that we could grow our own produce. We eventually found what seemed perfect: "It's a small house in a quiet area, and has lovely views from the garden," the owner told us on the 'phone. We had already planned a "house-hunting" day trip, so added that one to our list. It was the first we saw and, after viewing the rest, decided that it was what we were looking for.

We continued to live mainly in Portsmouth until the final decision to relocate was reached. Friends and relatives were surprised that we were moving to Wales; my brother thought we'd be back within the year! Selling the Portsmouth house proved to be easy, and within a couple of months we were moving with our last items of furniture and our two dogs, crossing the Severn Bridge.

Another community
This was going to be a new way of life for us both, living on a quiet mountain road on the outskirts of a small village with open country-side all around. I didn't realise quite how enclosed a community I would be living in again, until the day we took our dogs for a walk on the mountain. Two ladies, complete strangers, stopped to say hello. One asked us if we lived in the area.

"We have just moved permanently into our house in Rhiwfawr," I answered.

"Now, you two are interested in learning Welsh, aren't you? I've found out for you – the classes are in the village hall on Wednesday afternoons."

We thanked them and, wondering how they could possibly know anything about us, walked home, both amused and perplexed. Yes, such inquisitiveness existed in Portsmouth but perhaps not so openly expressed! We were made even more aware of the closeness of the community when our neighbour related some of the village history. Apparently, an ancestor of hers had owned a local quarry and built all of the houses on our road for his family. She is the last to live here – in the house in which she was born, which seems amazing. She and her husband have been wonderful neighbours to us, and there is no doubt that, if I am looking for perfect examples of Welshness, they embody its best aspects. Welsh speakers, they are obviously content with their life and home and yes, their national identity. They are openly proud of being Welsh, as I am proud of being English. You could probably sum up their Welshness as a quiet pride, totally at ease with who, what, and where they are.

During the last four years, there have been many events and incidents which have prompted thoughts about Wales and Welshness. I have gradually come to realise that, if you take away the obvious difference of nationality, there is not much that is fundamentally different between the people of Wales and England.

So, where do I stand in all of this? It must be said that, although there are strong similarities between my childhood community and my present environment, my identity is definitely steeped in England, as much as those who are born in Wales identify themselves with their country of birth, even though they may move away. Perhaps, then, you could define identity as something you are born with but through the years you add to, hopefully enriching that identity – and your life!

Dylan Thomas and Gwynfor Evans

by

CEFNFAB

IT CAN BE SAID THAT more books have been produced about Dylan Thomas, than the author himself has written. Here, however, is one morsel of information that has not been documented, which also magnifies this poetic genius' Welsh identity.

Let me explain at the outset that I never met Dylan Thomas. I was just seventeen when he died in nineteen fifty three at which time I did not even know of his existence. Then, about four years later, whilst preparing to go on the night shift at a local colliery, I heard "Under Milk Wood" for the very first time. I shall always remember how the voice of Richard Burton transfixed my entire being, and then how it echoed around my mind in unison with the sound of miners' mandrels hewing away at the coal.

The impact of hearing those words had left a profound impression, for immediately after work the following morning I journeyed to Swansea in order to purchase the book.

No, my interest in Dylan Thomas did not arise because it was fashionable to do so, for I have always truly admired his literature . . . and yet I believe there is a significant explanation as to why I feel so moved whenever I listen to the author's feverish words.

The environment from the moment of birth and on throughout life dictates one's sense of nationhood. Thus, it is feasible to believe that Thomas' refined language, which frequently refers to Wales, is steeped in his own rich Welsh background.* Not only does this manifest Thomas' profound feelings for his nation, but the author's

---

* Reference to Dylan Thomas' Welsh background on page 111.

words also awake a similar sensation within me whenever I read or hear his work.

Having studied the life and work of Dylan Thomas for nearly fifty years, as well as experiencing peoples' reaction to the subject, I have become gradually aware that other compatriots have similar nationalistic stirrings whenever they connect these feelings with the author's work. Indeed, I remember one occasion when a member of an audience stood up after listening to a story by Dylan and shouted out 'Wales for ever!' I have experienced other similar incidents, but none so poignant as what occurred during a celebratory event several years ago.

It was the year when Dr Gwynfor Evans won his initial parliamentary seat. His supporters, understandably, wanted to proclaim such a celebratory historical occasion. It was, after all, the first time that a Plaid Cymru candidate had entered the House of Commons. In order to mark the success, various events were organised throughout the constituency, one of them being a noson lawen in the locality where I lived.

Plaid Cymru in those days was a small party with very meagre revenue; therefore entertainers who would be willing to offer their services free of charge were sought.

I made it quite clear to the branch's secretary from the outset that I would be quite prepared to participate in their concert if I could present my work in English, the reason being that I had just learned a new piece and I wanted to practice it out in public for the first time. Having no bargaining power at his disposal, the organiser had no alternative but to agree.

The Pensioners' Hall in Brynaman was full to capacity, including several dignitaries. One of these was a Welsh radio commentator, who was, incidentally, the evening's master of ceremonies. Naturally, with him being in control of the proceedings, he inquired about my programme. I shall always remember – after I had informed him of my intended contribution – how he strode down to the front of the hall with an astonished look upon his face. He turned to the audience, whilst looking annoyingly at me from the corner of his eye, and proclaimed loudly at the same time that the next artist was to entertain them entirely in English. One can imagine, after such a hostile remark, that I was not greeted with any approving looks.

Slowly I gazed around at the inquiring faces until a complete hush had descended upon the hall. Then, after a long deliberate pause, I loudly announced that 'they could not have ice-cream every meal.'

I noticed from their startled expressions that my unexpected remark had taken their breath away; and before they had a chance to recover I was well away into the story. I vaguely sensed there was a gradual thaw to my frosty reception. The captivating words must have completely transformed their earlier opinion of having to sit and listen to an English literature presentation, for the applause that greeted the completion of the story was truly appreciative. It was not merely my interpretation of the tale that caused such a reaction, but the exquisite manner in which the author had composed the work. Could this also have been an ingredient of Welshness that they themselves had identified within their own feelings?

The true ultimate pleasure for me that evening, however, was not so much the applause that greeted my own performance, but what occurred immediately after the ovation.

Throughout his time at Westminster, Gwynfor Evans gained the respect of all the political parties. This was mainly due to the quiet, sincere and dignified manner he addressed the House of Commons, for his speeches always came direct from the heart. He also only spoke when he thought it absolutely necessary,

Therefore, I found it rather surprising to see Gwynfor standing after I had completed my rendering, for one does not usually expect an evening's honoured guest to speak at the end of an artist's performance. The audience themselves must have sensed the significance of the moment for a sudden silence fell upon the hall.

One can only reiterate Gwynfor's actual words, for they have a more meaningful ring when spoken in Welsh: "'Dw i erioed wedi clywed y Gymraeg mor glir yn yr Iaith Fain."

It must be said that Gwynfor Evans in making such a statement – that he had never heard Welshness so clearly expressed in English – was in itself remarkable.

Years earlier Gwynfor had severely reprimanded Dylan when the latter asked if he could join the Plaid Cymru party as a ploy to avoid enlistment during the Second World War. Therefore it would have been quite understandable for this distinguished gentleman to have ridiculed the person that he had once damned for being so 'unheroic.' But Gwynfor, of course, is an honourable man, for the words that he selects are always consistent with his own true feelings.

In this respect, there is no question as to his sincerity in proclaiming the accomplishment of Dylan Thomas' words. In so doing, not only did he affirm that the author's literature was typically Welsh, but it also reveals Gwynfor Evans' own Welsh identity. Surely it can be said that honesty of expression is yet another virtue that characterises the people of Wales?

The Welsh Gentry, 1750-1850

by

BRIAN DAVIES
(Ystradgynlais)

THE LANDOWNING CLASS known as the Gentry had by 1750 firmly established itself in South Wales, and virtually ruled every facet of its everyday life.

Their political and social aspiration by then was to emulate the English way of life of their peers. They applied it to their estates and their tenant farmers and to the workforce in general. This policy was to continue and grow for the next ninety years or so, which led to a disastrous conclusion.

The social order was: firstly, the Squire himself, the lesser landowners called the 'Squireens'; the magistrates, without exception from one of the above, or the Clergy, and men of independent means who were described as 'Gentlemen'.

The magistrates were very powerful men indeed who set the *rents, wages, food prices and other such commodities in the area,* whilst they also sat in judgement at court on wrongdoers.

The magistrates, often father and son, were the sole judges on cases where they themselves had an interest. They looked on a day at court as a day out, and it is on record that cases often had to be adjourned as the magistrates were too intoxicated to continue after a long lunch. Many a man was tried and sentenced in a language he barely understood or not at all, and informed of his punishment outside the court later. An example of theft was seven years hard labour for as little as stealing a pocket watch. This was a harsh and unjust system which continued for many years and was known to the population as *'Justice's Justice'.*

The Clergy were more often than not from the landed class, and were looked upon by the people with great distrust and seen as the agents of the Gentry. The tithe taxes and other levies imposed by the Church of England caused much resentment and bitterness among the community, many of whom were Non Conformist and resented paying taxes to provide the vicar with a living. So unpopular was the Church of England in many parts of Wales that it was commonly known in Welsh as yr "Hen Estrones" or "Hen Fam" (stranger or old mother) and as Non Conformity rapidly grew it became ever more despised in many areas.

The Squires over the years were becoming more and more Anglicised and a growing chasm was developing between them and the people who stubbornly continued to live their Welsh way of life. In fact some became figures of fun amongst the locals as the Gentry invented false family histories, and a plain John Jones would overnight appear as Iohan Fitzsimons or Furqhuar and toured the district making complete and utter fools of themselves in the eyes of the populace, who looked upon these antics with great merriment. But, of course, there was a serious side to all this as the landowners fell deeply into debt by emulating the English, as they did not have the resources to do so. Many large estates were re-mortgaged and, to claw the money back to pay for their follies, they doubled and trebled the tenants' rent, causing great distress and misery and near starvation in many cases. There were many evictions for non payment of rent. New tenants were brought in, only to fail as their predecessors did to keep to their agreement. The process, of course, would begin all over again. This method was known as Rent Racking, and as there was no redress in law the poor people were helpless to prevent it.

The Landowners were by now becoming hated figures in the community through their methods of extracting money. The pot was starting to boil over as deep resentment and anger grew all over South Wales. It eventually exploded in the form of the Chartist Movement in the Eastern Industrial areas, and the Rebecca Riots in the rural areas of the West. These two actions were about to shake the Establishment to its very foundations. It is more than likely that this prompted the Reverend Fleming Gough, Vicar and Squire of the Ynyscedwyn Estate at Ystradgynlais, to write to the Land Office around this period of time. In his letter he stated that the agricultural classes were wretched and utterly distressed. In another letter to another priest at Cil-y-bebyll Parish, he stated his intention of paying him a visit, but would have to return home before dark owing to the hostility of the natives. The Gentry were by now becoming very concerned at the social climate which they had created by their abysmal treatment of the population. The poverty and the depravity that was rampant in society was now beginning to haunt them. They did not have to wait very long for the reaction.

The peasantry (Y Werin) of South Wales were by and large a peaceable and respectful people with a keen sense of duty, and loyalty to their masters. They were also in the main deeply religious with a Bible in most homes, and had deep knowledge of the scriptures. Those who could not read learned them by heart in Sunday Schools which were by now emerging.

In their hour of need they turned to the Bible for inspiration, and the name Rebecca became the symbol of their fight against the oppression they were being subjected to. The Rebecca Riots will go down in history as the turning point in the rule of the Gentry in South Wales. Quite simply the people said enough was enough, the result being that they rioted by smashing the tollgates on the Turnpike roads and set fire to haystacks and other belongings of the Gentry, who were shocked and frightened at these events. These rural despots ultimately panicked by bringing in troops and police to quell the rioters. This, however, proved to be of no avail, for these forces of 'law and order' were led a merry dance around the country lanes, and made to look very foolish indeed. The few that were caught and brought to Court were mostly released for lack of evidence. An incident at Hendy near Pontarddulais resulted in the death of a seventy-six year old female tollgate keeper, Hannah Williams. Police and soldiers at the scene had set a trap which led to the capture of some of the rioters. The resulting trial held at Cardiff saw men convicted and sentenced to as many as twenty years penal servitude in Australia, although it was never proved who fired the fatal shot. This action, along with some other factors, brought an end to the Rebecca Riots.

Following these events a Government enquiry was set up, which lasted for several months. Evidence was gathered from all corners of South Wales. Many of the wrongs that were done to the people were exposed. From that point on the absolute power of the Landed Gentry was on the wane and was virtually gone by the end of the Nineteenth Century.

The one factor that stands out clearly during this stressful and turbulent period in our history is that the ordinary Welsh people kept their identity totally intact, whilst the Landed Gentry lost theirs forever.

Llwynrhydowen

by

CEFNFAB

IT HAS OFTEN BEEN said that Wales is one large village. Visitors from another country find it very strange, if not amusing, that one knows so many ordinary people from various parts of the principality. Therefore, it goes without saying that there is a close sense of affinity between the country's people. If a person, for example, is in strife or real need, then members of the community will rally around to support that family. This communal support is very much a Welsh characteristic that has been evident in Wales throughout the ages – and the Nineteenth Century in particular.

Life in rural parts of Cardiganshire was an ongoing struggle during the days when squires were the dominant rulers of their estates. The tenants were literally controlled 'limb and soul' by the landed gentry, for they were not allowed to voice any opinion that would be detrimental to their masters' interest. One such squire was J. D. Lloyd Davies of Allt-yr-Odyn Estate, near Llwynrhydowen, located in the county's heartland. Even the village's minister, Gwilym Marles,* and his entire congregation were thrown out of chapel because they did not conform to the Squire's views and practices.

It must be said at the outset, that the person responsible for causing such upheaval in the area was his agent, J. Mason Allen. (Eventually it was revealed that this was due to a selfish interest, so the latter could then schemingly acquire his master's wealth). Through being in a continual drunken stupor, the Squire was never in a true fit state of mind to realise how much Llwynrhydowen's wretched souls were suffering under his tyrannical agent. Families

---

* See page 111.

were evicted from their homes when they could not meet extortionate rents. It could be said, however, that there was one such family who suffered even more than the other wretched victims of the area.

John and Mary Jones had seven children and they lived in the farmstead of Ffynnonllywelyn. During the period of their eviction notice, four of their youngest ones perished of diphtheria. The remaining children were so despondent with what had happened in their lives that all three said they would migrate to America. The parents, having already lost four of their young ones, decided that they would also leave Wales with the surviving children.

One autumn evening, prior to their departure, a large number of the community had gathered in Ffynnonllywelyn's court yard. This kind of occurrence was usual, as it was a Welsh tradition to give a communal send off to whoever moved far away from their home. Good wishes echoed around the nearby pastures as families bid their last farewells; whilst, of course, there were also singing and tears.

The following morning, Dafydd and Mary Jones and their three children commenced their journey to America. They stayed the first evening at Carmarthen before eventually travelling on to Liverpool. Soon after the ship had left the Lancashire port one of the sons was taken seriously ill. Then, within a week, his brother also found himself in the same delirious condition. It was when the ship was approaching New York that they noticed the daughter had the same feverish symptoms as her brothers. All three children were taken to a sanatorium at Blackwell Island, near the Hudson River. They were never seen again, for there they died of an infectious decease. (The three children had been contaminated with small pox whilst they stayed in a house at Carmarthen.)

The parents, understandably, were broken-hearted. Having lost their three surviving children, there was no purpose for them then to stay on in America and so they returned to their homeland for solace.

It is said that bad news travels fast, for even before the bereaved couple's arrival a large number of relatives and friends had gathered at Llandysul station to share their sorrow. In the true Welsh tradition of helping fellow countrymen to overcome their difficulties, a warm-hearted squire from Bronwydd heard of their plight and gave them a smallholding. This, sadly, did not free the grief within the mother's soul, for she soon returned to the fields of Ffynnon-llywelyn . . . searching and crying out for her lost children.

The Great Escape

by

MARJORIE SHOWALLA

IT WAS NINETEEN FIFTY-TWO and in those days not many people left the Welsh valleys. In my youth I had served behind the counter of the local Co-op during the war. Therefore, as most of the community knew me, I was given a farewell concert as they would to the soldiers before their departure.

As I was sitting on the stage of the local miners' welfare hall, it suddenly occurred to me that I was *really* going far, far away and leaving my home in Wales forever . . . but forty-five years hence is another story.

I met Hasson my husband in London whilst I was nursing, and there were married. Hasson had come to this country as a student from *Aden*. Then, after completing his training, he had to return to serve his own people. I was rather apprehensive about leaving, but yet I was full of romantic ideas about sand, sea and moonlit Arabian nights.

My husband – although rather shy – had put on a brave face for my sake as he sat on the stage that evening. As I gazed down on the people in the hall a lump came to my throat, for I felt unhappy about leaving my friends. Hasson saw the tears in my eyes and squeezed my hand as if to say 'don't worry, everything will be all right'.

We left Wales on a bright sunny day in May before eventually arriving in *Aden*. Hasson was very excited to meet his family again. I, myself, a young nurse from the Welsh valleys, was venturing into the unknown. I could not have imagined what was ahead of us as I stepped down from the plane during that time in nineteen fifty-two.

Aden was a colony in South Arabia, which at the time was governed by Britain and where my husband and I would live for the next sixteen years. I thought that it would be an Arabian romantic adventure until it all came to a tragic end in November nineteen sixty-seven. What happened then soon proved to be an unbelievable experience!

By this time we had built a house in *Khormaksar*, not knowing at the time that eventually this house would become a shelter for fugitives before it was taken over by the government.

I was now able to speak Arabic and was working in a clinic at a place called *Malla*.

The trouble began when two sectors fought each other for the control of *Aden* when the colony was handed over from the British. One sector was the *Adenis* Arabs, many of which were educated in Britain. The other sector included Bedouins, mostly from the protectorate of *Aden* who were uneducated as well as being communists.

The *Adenis* were quite surprised when the British handed over the colony to the communist Bedouins. Before independence the Arabs had been fighting the British troops and therefore it had now become dangerous to go anywhere. Due to this mounting tension, we decided to send our children to my parents in Wales for safety.

Then in November nineteen sixty-seven, it all came to an abrupt end. One fellow from Port Trust was machine-gunned and his body – along with thirteen others – was dumped on *Abian* beach. That night we both stayed with a friend in a place called *Crater*, for we were terrified of going home. On November the second and Friday the third there was an almighty battle at a place called *Sheikh-othman* and *Al-mansura*. Many hundreds of people were killed.

Although it was Hasson's day off, he decided on the Friday to help at the hospital, where he heard that educated *Adenis* Arabs were all going to be slaughtered. The following day my husband was admitted to the hospital as a patient for safety. Then he telephoned me that evening to say that the 'situation had become desperate' and to try and find a way for us to get out of *Aden*.

Early Monday morning a relative came knocking at the gate at 6 a.m. with all his family packed into a small car. They had come from *Al-mansura*. Many houses were bombed whilst several people were also killed that night. The place had been surrounded by fighting Arabs.

On Sunday I went to the hospital, and even though I was a trained nurse I felt very sick when I saw all the carnage there that morning. Then, early on Monday, my husband rang me to say that one of his friends was brought into the hospital decapitated and that his own name was on the list for the same treatment. He emphasized how desperate it was for me to find a way for us to get out.

Europeans were not allowed out that day, for there was a curfew on at the time. In spite of that I rushed to *Steamer Point* where the *Stalko* travelling office was situated, in order for me to get a passage out of *Aden* for my husband.

I was taken there in a friend's battered old car. On the roofs of nearby buildings I could see snipers, who, when they saw me, shouted: "Get the bloody hell out of here!!"

And it *was* 'bloody hell' with guns firing in all directions. The only hope I thought I had was that my nurse's uniform would deter them from shooting at me.

The shipping agent, whom I knew, gave me his last ticket for the plane to *Jubouti*. This, he said, was a mark of his gratitude when I invited him over to Wales a few years previously. He remembered the welcome my parents had given him. (Ie, ma' croeso'r Cymry yn heli i bob drwg.) Then he advised me to go and collect my visa at the French Embassy, which was inside the barracks in *Steamer Point*.

There was a young soldier at the gate, who insisted that he would shoot me if I entered the barracks because I had no pass. The poor young lad did not know what to do when I told him:

"Then, go ahead and shoot!"

He eventually let me pass.

The ambassador refused at first to give me a visa, until I informed him that I would not move from the place until I was given one. Yes, I stubbornly stood my ground until he eventually gave me a visa for two days only.

Tuesday arrived and my husband at long last was on the plane to *Jubouti*. In his company were several other *Adenis*, and also my husband's cousin, whom we had secretly hidden in the flat upstairs with fourteen other fugitives. It could be said that our house resembled a transit camp.

On Thursday the communists watched the airports. Two people from upstairs were caught and taken to prison. They now started watching ports to catch people leaving, for they had already taken three off the ships before they sailed.

My husband had booked passages for us on a ship SS *Balkan*, whose first port of call was to be at *Jubouti* then *Aden*. My husband had decided to board this ship, which eventually brought him back to *Aden*. This was a 'dicey' thing to do.

I continued to work in the clinic in *Malla*. It had entered my mind that they might even take me as a hostage to lure my husband back.

Eventually the ship came to *Aden* on Saturday at 4 a.m. with my husband on board. I had sent the luggage on to the ship with my father-in-law. My friend in the shipping agency had already arranged that if he told me on the phone to call at his office on Monday, that this then would really mean Sunday. Precaution such as this had to be taken because my telephone was tapped. People would often telephone me to ask where my husband was. I, of course, kept giving them different answers.

I had arranged to be picked up at the clinic at 10 am on Sunday by a friend who once used to drive the children to school. He was only too willing to help – especially as he himself had been imprisoned by the 'enemy'.

I went to work as usual. Then, at precisely 10 a.m., I just calmly walked out of the clinic without uttering a word – even a good-bye to those whom I had come to know so well. This was so different to the goodbyes I received when I left Wales. My heart was sad as I found my way to the ship to join my husband. The captain, after much coaxing, and the dangers pointed out to him, omitted my husband's name from the passenger list. I am sure he eventually realised the threat to his own safety if the authorities learned of my husband's presence on board his ship. We were both locked in our cabin until we sailed away to freedom at 9 p.m. on Monday. The last few hours – just waiting there and not knowing whether they would come to pick us up at any time – was the most dreadful experience of my life.

We sighed with relief when the ship sailed out of Aden. Then, with sheer nervous exhaustion, we both fell into a welcoming sleep.

In *Aden* at that particular time, there were approximately five hundred people killed and several hundreds injured. It was a *real* blood-bath. The smell of death was everywhere, whilst its presence could also be sensed in people's despairing faces.

Wives searching for missing husbands, mothers praying for lost sons, whilst women in their sorrow shredded their clothes and wept . . . Thank God we got away from it all and were on our way back to Wales!

Warmth

by

JEAN E. WILLIAMS

AFTER LEAVING our happy RAF days behind us, Charlie and I had settled somewhat into the tiny Liverpool suburb town of Prenton. I began to wonder how the civilian way of life would affect me. Throughout my first twenty-eight years I had not experienced anything but the forces, as my father was also a serving airman.

It had been one of those glorious late spring days. I relished the refreshing breeze that blew in from Wales over the Dee Estuary. There was nothing more welcoming than cool English air after Singapore's sultry heat. Although I enjoyed my three years there with the RAF, nothing was better than coming home again and seeing the surrounding shores of England.

Sounds of honking cars and the alarming realisation that our marriage had turned sour, all contributed to my mind's disturbed state. I just had to run away . . . But how could I do that, for I was on my way to collect our two lovely young daughters from their new school?

Upon reaching the school I vaguely heard a pleasant voice greeting me with a 'good afternoon'. I turned around to see a middle aged woman smiling at me, whom I recognised from my previous visits to the school. One did not have an opportunity to speak to her as the children by this time were racing out of the classrooms, so I acknowledged her considerate regard with a polite nod. If the occasion ever arose, I thought, I should perhaps introduce myself to her.

On my arrival at the school the following morning, there was no sign of the lady I was seeking. The children who were with her the previous day were accompanied by another person. Somewhat disappointed, I trudged begrudgingly back to my lonely house. Charlie hadn't come home for two days, although I suppose by this time I had come acquainted with his stories and excuses. There was no need for me to be told, for I knew full well he had been with one of his lady friends.

As I sat, a forlorn figure in the back room of our home, I could not hinder the tears which dampened my cheeks. Through an aquatic forming mist I attempted to read the local newspaper. Gradually they cleared well enough for me to see an advert in one of the pages. A well known cosmetic firm was seeking a representative to work in the area where I lived. Abounded by relief, I suddenly felt a sense of pressure being released from my mind, which can best be described as a few fleeting seconds of escapism. In those few brief moments, I thought to myself: 'I'm sure I could do something like that.' I'll telephone at once, before another person applies for the vacancy.

A few days later I commenced as a sales cosmetic representative. 'My loneliness is at its end,' I thought, 'for I shall now meet new people.' This flare of hope, however, was soon extinguished through having to constantly march towards unresponsive closed doors. 'Oh,' I thought, as I knocked for the umpteenth time, 'how long will I be able to survive this torture? I wish I could go home and ease the pain of my burning feet.' Then, as I was in the process of conceding to my futile errant, the closed door suddenly opened.

I was pleased to recognise the young woman who answered my knock, for I'd seen her at the school on several occasions.

"Hello," I said anxiously, "would you like to buy some cosmetics?"

"No, thank you," she replied in a pleasant voice, "but wait a moment, my mother might be interested. I'll go and get her for you."

"Don't leave the lady standing there", said a friendly voice beyond the door, "invite her in." I recognised her as soon as I entered the house. Yes, she was the very same person whom I'd seen the other day – the friendly one by the school gates.

Before I had the opportunity of explaining the purpose of my visit I was asked, "would you like to take some weight off your feet and have a cup of tea?" Never have I appreciated a beverage so much than the one I received on that tiring afternoon whilst selling cosmetics in the Wirral. Not only was I grateful for the tea itself, but to be able to sit down and relax in the company of such a pleasant lady was sheer relief.

Her name was Mrs. Storey, but she said for me to call her Phoebe. I could not understand at the time why she had been so friendly, until it was explained to me a few weeks later.

"I hope you won't mind me saying this to you, my love, but I've been concerned since I first saw you outside the school. You always looked so sad and your eyes seemed to have a distant gaze in them."

Phoebe became not only one of my best customers, but eventually proved to be a very good friend. She would often invite me back to her home after I left the children at school. Over numerous cups of tea I poured out my heart. She was so sympathetic and such a good listener. The sharing of my problems with her was truly halved. Their release for another person to hear made me feel less a prisoner of my mind. I also came to know Phoebe much better. She informed me her father had come to Liverpool years earlier to seek work and that he was Welsh.

"I remember how much his stories about Wales meant to me as a child. The place of dragons and high mountains and where women wore high hats and where also there was always singing."

"I've never thought of going to Wales, for to me it was just another part of England which made up the UK."

"No, no, dear, it is a country with its own identity. The Welsh are a very friendly lot, you know, like one large family."

"Yes, being in the RAF was something like that. Oh, if I could only still be part of it all."

"There, there, don't fret. Let me be an extended member of your family."

It was only then I realised that consideration towards other people's welfare was a truly Welsh identity, through Phoebe herself being so friendly.

The local library was very near where I lived. I remember going there one day just to idle my time away. It was more in desperation to avoid my loneliness at home than to search for a book. Then, as I gazed along the numerous volumes on the shelves, a title suddenly caught my eye: *Romance in the Welsh Mountains*. Little did I realise it then, but this book's name would have a significant meaning for me during the forthcoming weeks.

The story was about a young woman who had similar troubled experiences as my own, who went to Wales and fell in love with a stranger. I initially only read the first two paragraphs. The tormenting thoughts that ran through my mind at the time did not allow such luxury as to sit down and enjoy a novel.

Things were getting from bad to worse at home as I desperately thought of a way out from my dilemma. I just could not accept that my husband of seven wedded – and what I had always believed to be blissful years – had betrayed me. One assumes that whenever a marriage breaks down there is usually 'a fly in the ointment'. This time, however, I was the fly caught up in a web of deceit. Yes, the 'spider' on this occasion was my husband's bit on the side, who, incidentally, had deceitfully woven her way into our home. Yet, I believed however entangled my life seemed to be, it could not be compared with the mess existing within his mind. How could he hope to gain any form of happiness, whilst abandoning two beautiful little girls? Money was really short and I couldn't survive on my pin-money job, for Charlie rarely gave me any meaningful housekeeping. There was no alternative; I'd have to look for a full-time job.

One day, as I glanced through the pages of a local newspaper, an advertisement caught my eye. A holiday camp in North Wales required staff with some clerical experience. 'This could very well be the opportunity I've been seeking,' I thought, 'for I was a typist whilst serving in the RAF.' I applied for the post, and to my astonishment an interview was arranged almost immediately. They informed me after reaching the appointed venue, 'I would be working in one of their staff offices as a secretary and how soon could I start?'

"Does this mean . . .?"

"Yes, you are appointed."

I hurriedly contacted my mother, revealing to her my dire circumstances. In hearing the sympathetic tone of her voice on the telephone, I knew she would look after the girls until 'I sorted myself out'.

The phone call came after three days. A young man's voice informed me the coach would be leaving Liverpool on Monday at ten in the morning and would I be there?

The tenth of August nineteen seventy shall always be a day clasped within my thoughts. Looking out through the coach window as it left the city on that dismal, overcast morning, I thought how well it matched my feelings. 'Why, oh, why did it have to happen?' These haunting problems were usually other people's baggage. I was merely a victim of remorse, huddled in a seat too exhausted to cry. The tears that once streamed down my cheeks had now completely dried.

Until then my entire life had revolved around that charlatan and our charming daughters of six and five years of age. I shall always remember how my solicitor's words reverberated harshly in my ears, when he advised me to vacate our marital home. He told me I should do this immediately before commencing divorce proceedings. Even though I fully understood the logic of this procedure, it still did not resolve any of the problems. Neither was it an instantaneous remedy to my inner despair.

In desperation I considered revenge, in the hope it would quell the mounting anger in my soul. Then after giving thought to the outcome of murder, the flame of reprisal was soon distinguished. How could I engineer such a conclusion, and in so doing allow my children to be parentless? Suicide, therefore, was no longer an alternative. Such was my dilemma, until Fate kindly led me by its hand.

My kind, sympathetic mother, how could I ever thank her for offering to look after the babes until I could sort out my tangled life? It was only for six weeks, so I'd soon see my little girls again.

A few hours later, as the coach made its way through the North Wales countryside and pass unpronounceable place-names, I thought of Phoebe. This was the country she had so often explained to me

– the beauty of the scenery and warmth of its people. But how could this resolve my problems? I asked myself as we arrived at our destination.

Dreary eyed, with the faces of my children continually revolving around in my mind, I stumbled wearily off the bus to the jolting presence of a holiday atmosphere. Even though my children were constantly in my thoughts, it was memories of my late teen years that came flooding back. They were not warm reminisces, but cold distant ones as our names were called out in the camp's reception office. Surely, this can't be the country that Phoebe so often described, for the warmth one expected, was absent within the curtly greetings of these people.

"Jean Allen?"

"Yes," I replied.

"Your chalet is in row D, number 8."

I was then given a key and told to start work in the staff offices at eight the following morning. When I heard those regimental instructions being directed at me, I could only think of the time when I first joined the RAF. In those days I didn't feel so forlorn, for all the other recruits were in the same situation. Here, however, the circumstances were somewhat different.

It didn't take me long to find the chalet where I was placed. The room was pokey, dark and musty, which immediately added to my gloom . . . knowing I was to share it with no one but my own miserable self. Despairingly, I banged my head against the flaking yellow coloured wall until I felt quite dizzy. Then, in gazing up at the ceiling, I suddenly thought I had inflicted damage to my brain. Glaring down at me from above was a large horrendous spider whose advancing dive made me imagine that I was being attacked by a vindictive Jezebel. How was I to sleep in here tonight? I had no doubt I was standing at death's door, until I heard the laughter of children from outside the building. This brought me back to my senses, which immediately made me think of my own darling girls. Six weeks would soon pass and then we would be together. Oh! If only I could save enough money for the three of us to have a little place and be a happy family once again.

'I shall not allow this gloom to conquer me,' I stubbornly thought. 'Surely, the girls will be missing me by now, so I must write to each one and say how much I miss and love them.' After the letters were completed, I ventured out into the warm August evening to look for a letter-box, which I saw gleaming in the distance. Little did I know then, but my entire life was soon going to change when I decided to go out and post that mail.

Oh, I thought as the letters disappeared into the mouth of the letter-box, if only I could be whisked away in their company and reach my daughters tomorrow. Then, suddenly from behind me, I heard a deep, rich, Welsh voice:

"Hello, staff or holiday maker?"

Momentarily perturbed, I slowly turned around. A silhouetting shadow stood out between me and the glaring sunset. After focusing on the figure for a few moments, I discovered it was a young man with a bushy beard. He had sad green eyes, although his smile was consistent and attractive.

The stranger soon informed me that he was working in the camp's bar. Then, in a polite transaction of words, I informed him that I'd just arrived and would be working in the staff offices. Out of the corner of my eye I saw him gazing at me shyly before drawing a deep breath:

"Would you like to see the chair-lifts?"

I pondered for a while if I should go – but he seemed so nice. Anyhow my life was at its lowest ebb, so damn it, what did I have to lose?

"Yes," I suddenly replied, "I might as well."

After only five minutes of exchanging information about ourselves, I felt as if we had known each other for years – especially as our circumstances were so similar. Then he made the most unexpected remark:

"We might as well get married."

"Why not," I replied, "but I don't even know your name."

Upon wakening the next morning, I thought it had all been a dream. I didn't feel like any breakfast, so after a sip of water I went to find out where I would be working.

The morning went by quickly finding out how things ran in the office, whilst also reading the staff rules. Yet, at the same time, I was keeping an eye out for my saviour. Then, at one o'clock, as previously arranged, he was standing there in front of me, smiling. I thought his eyes had a glint of hope, without the tint of sadness that they contained the previous evening.

"Dinner?" he asked hesitatingly. "It's time for us to go to the canteen."

After we were beyond the office girls' prying eyes, he gently took my hand. It could be said, sharing each other's company in the canteen that afternoon, was far more nourishing than our meal. The initial intention in coming to this holiday camp was to seek refuge from the turmoil that existed in both of our lives. The same evening, as I am sure one now will anticipate, we decided to do a flit from the camp. I did not hesitate to do so, especially after hearing the promise contained within these words.

"I know where there's a little bungalow for rent. It's quite near my mother's place in South Wales."

Dafydd had such trusting eyes. I must take a chance on this man, I thought. He's gorgeous . . . and he is Welsh.

Early, the following morning, we sneaked out of the sleeping camp in his rusty bucket of a car, which rattled its way along winding countryside roads to our future destiny – a small bungalow situated in one of the valleys of South Wales.

Over the next few days, we emulsioned all the rooms and turned the tiny bungalow into a cosy love nest. Yet, there was still a vacuum in my heart, which Dafydd fully realised. He held me gently in his arms and said:

"Now that we have a nice home, let us go and collect your girls."

During those unforgettable moments I felt a warm glow more penetrating even than the heat of Singapore. The dawn of those undetectable rays were a shaft of realisation within my mind, for the book that I commenced reading recently had eventually been completed in my very own 'Romance in the Welsh Mountains'.

A Shot in the Dark

by

LEON

IT IS ESSENTIAL, in order that a miner survives the harshness of a colliery environment, for him to obtain a diet of black humour, especially stories related in the coalmines of South Wales. Here is such a tale that can be identified as being of typical Welsh wit.

The coal fire was roaring up the chimney of the rather antiquated, electrical repair shop. I was grateful for the warmth of its flames as it was a bitterly cold January night. I felt a very grown up eighteen year old, as it was my first night shift stint as an electrical apprentice at Cae-glas Colliery. One of the first memories I had, as a child, was gazing at my father in wonder and awe whenever he returned home from the colliery. His face always seemed to have been a blackened mask, and his sweat- stained brow signified a strenuous night's work at the pit. I shall always remember him saying as a smile rippled across his face. "The cats and criminals shift, that's what they call night work you know, boy." . . . Now I was doing exactly what my own dad had done.

Llew, the electrician, to whom I was assigned, was sleeping soundly in the anteroom. I had often heard about his slumbering habits, through drink, from the other men. Judging by the state of him at the beginning of the shift, it was quite apparent that he had also drunk a few earlier that evening.

"I'm going to get my head down for a few hours," he had announced tipsily. "Carry on with your work and wake me up if there's a problem."

Fortunately, the night shift was generally regarded as the easiest of the three shifts and electricians did not venture underground unless there was an emergency, such as a breakdown. I busied myself doing the work allocated. At around mid-shift the main door of the shop was thrown open and a giant of a man stood on the threshold. It was Bryn Mawr the surface overman. Although he was a neighbour of mine, we had never spoken a word to each other in all the years I had known him. He had a reputation, within the village, as a wife beater. Indeed, the best recollection I ever had of him was that he always represented a Pariah-like figure within our community. His face now bore a dour expression, his eyes were unsmiling and he gave no sign of recognition.

"Where's Llew?" he demanded.

I had to think fast. I was no snitch and knew full well that if he had seen Llew in such a drunken state it would have meant his cards.

"He's gone underground on a call" I replied, diffidently.

"Then what are *you* doing here?" His eyes held mine, waiting for the reply. I felt like a victim of the Spanish Inquisition. I would have to be careful, very careful of what I said next, for he was a dangerous adversary.

"He asked me to stay here and keep an eye on the workshop in case any of the tools get pinched."

It sounded lame, pathetic really, but it was the best I could come up with at such short notice. I was fast becoming an accomplished liar.

"Did he indeed," he snorted contemptuously and then, suddenly, changed tack.

"No matter, lad, you'll do. I want you to come with me to the railway sidings and bring that big electrical drill with you." He pointed to the largest, weightiest drill we had in stock. I would have loved to have told him that it wasn't my job or that he wasn't my line manager, but to do so would have thrown the spotlight back on the whereabouts of the 'Sleeping Beauty'. I wanted to avoid that at all costs.

A minute later we were on our way. A biting, easterly wind blew straight off the common, taking my breath away at times. It was a moonless night with Orion already striding the Milky Way, off, yet again, on another hunting foray through the eternity of time and space. At that particular moment I wished that I could have accompanied him.

Bryn set off at a brisk pace whilst I brought up the rear, carrying this hulking piece of machinery. We were about half way there when my shoulder began to hurt abominably with the weight of the drill and I began to lag behind. Eventually, Bryn looked back and saw that I was struggling.

"Hurry up lad!" He demanded. The bloody shift will be over by the time we get there." He made no attempt to relieve me of the load or to give a helping hand. He was either unaware or impervious to my suffering. I suspected the latter. I was determined not to show any sign of weakness so, with gritted teeth and a redoubling of effort, I eventually reached the destination.

I took in the scene immediately. Under the powerful lights of the sidings stood a solitary, wooden coal truck with its side hatches drawn upwards, revealing that it was fully laden. Adjacent to this coal wagon was a bunker with a conveyor belt running directly underneath. Half a dozen washery employees were present, huddled together for warmth. They had obviously been trying to empty the contents of the truck into the bunker and thereby to the belt, in order that it could be transported for screening. They had failed with shovels and bars for the simple reason that the coal had frozen into a solid mass inside. Now I knew why he wanted the drill.

Bryn was in his element as he barked out orders at the men.

"I want four holes drilled. Here! Here! Here! And here! He chalked what he thought were strategic points in the mass of coal. Then, obediently, the men went about their task, whilst I, an exhausted, frozen bystander, viewed the proceedings. Within a quarter of an hour or so, four neat holes had been bored.

"Better put a cap* in each hole just to loosen the coal, like," ventured Twm Bach. Twm had worked underground for countless years as a collier, until ill health had forced him to seek employment in the washery. He knew a thing or two about coal did Twm.

"Don't talk so bloody daft, mun, Bryn snarled. Caps will never loosen it. I'm going to put half a pound in each hole. That should do it nicely," he added. There were gasps from the men.

* Detonator.

"Have it your own way," uttered Twm resignedly.

Finally, preparations were complete and we all retired to a safe distance behind a corrugated iron shed.

"All clear!!" yelled Bryn. "FIRE!!!" There was a resounding *BOOM*. The front of the shed was peppered with flying debris and then silence, an eerie silence, the same kind of hush that is heard outside the colliery office when men open their pay packets. After a few seconds we rushed, as a man, to the site of the explosion. Nothing could be seen for a while then the smoke and dust slowly began to settle. I stared in utter disbelief at what I saw, eventually, manifest itself. I thought at first that my eyes were playing tricks, and it was a mirage of some sort. But, even with a rather sketchy grasp of general knowledge, I knew that a mirage occurred in the heart of a blazing desert not in the heart of the Upper Swansea Valley on a winter's night

Where once stood a proud coal truck now only its skeletal remains bore testament that it had existed at all. Four wheels and two axles, still quivering slightly with the force of the explosion, were all that was left. Of its contents and the wooden sideboards there was no sign. They had been blown to the four corners of Comin y Cannon.

"Arglwydd Mawr, beth yffarn sy' wedi digwydd 'ma?" said Bryn in a trembling voice.

I had an overwhelming urge to laugh. I did my best to stifle the chortle, for I knew, if Bryn had heard it, it would have landed me in big trouble. I needn't have worried. The humour of the situation was not lost on the men. Within a few seconds the air was filled with a huge chorus of mirth and laughter. Tears rolled aimlessly down our cheeks, whilst everyone's sides were splitting. The amusing scene was truly infectious. Every one joined in . . . except, of course, Bryn Mawr.

"I don't see anything to bloody laugh at. We'd better try shifting this lot off the line before the day shift starts or we're all in trouble." He was back on even keel again.

"*We're* in trouble?" asked Twm Bach. There was a bite to his tone. "You're in trouble, you mean. This is your f****** doing, mun. I tried to tell you. But, oh no! you wouldn't listen to me. Determined to have your own way as bloody usual. You've blown it this time, I can tell you!" There was a fresh howl of laughter as the men seized on the pun, intended or otherwise. "And just how do you think we're goin' to move it, eh? Skyhooks is it? No! We're going back to the washery and the young lad here is going back to the shop. You sort out your own f****** mess."

"Bryn will have to pay for all the coal he blew up," croaked Danny Double Take. With his beak – like nose and, huge, blood-shot eyes, he presented quite an alarming spectacle as he gazed, balefully, at Bryn from beneath his balaclava. It was rumoured, amongst the men, that Danny's wife stopped him going out after four o'clock in the winter in case his appearance should frighten the younger kids on the street. I didn't believe *that one*.

"I wonder how much a ton of coal costs these days?" he mused. Whether it was meant in a rhetorical sense I wasn't sure, but the rest of the men evidently didn't think so.

"About fifteen quid a ton, I reckon," said Twm. "The truck was a sixteen tonner, so that would be . . ." There was a silence, with much furrowing of brows and counting of fingers as the group grappled with the niceties of mental multiplication. I prided myself at being fairly good with figures and, within a few seconds, had the answer, but kept very quiet. A 'know it all' had a habit of becoming a nasty cropper at Cae-glas. A few minutes elapsed with no answer forthcoming from the group.

"That's two hundred and forty pounds," I blurted out. I couldn't help it. They could have been there until the day shift came in.

"That's right lad," said Twm. "I had just come to that figure myself. Waiting for someone to say it first, like."

"Then there's the cost of the truck, and that's got to be at least a hundred quid." This came from Evan Lovely Boy, Cae-glas' answer to Rock Hudson.

This time the men were 'on the ball'.

"That's *three* hundred and forty quid," they sang out, almost in harmony. Obviously, mental addition was more to their liking.

In a Welsh mining environment ribbing and teasing were all part of everyday life. It was this banter that helped disguise the dangers, the harshness of the conditions and, somehow, made the shift more palatable. You had to learn to take it and dish it out, or boy, you were a 'gonner'! In this case, though, it was more than just banter, there was an acrimonious edge to it, due, no doubt, to Bryn's character and demeanour.

"Do you think that he'll have to pay in one lump-sum or will they allow him to pay weekly for it?"

"Definitely in one lump-sum. The Coal Board will want to recover the loss immediately."

"I can see the 'Bwms'* at his door now. I wonder if they'll take the three-piece suite or the double bed first?"

And so the baiting went on and on.

The change that had come over Bryn was remarkable. The arrogant, overbearing demeanour had disappeared as if it never existed. He sank to his haunches with his head buried in his hands.

"Oh Duw! Duw! O'r Arglwydd sy'n gwbod!" He groaned, at no one in particular. There followed a torrent of Anglo-Saxon, four-letter expletives. Then . . .

"Oh, mam fach! Beth ddiawl fi mynd i 'neud nawr?" He was, obviously, in purgatory itself and 'cracking up' under the strain. Perhaps, in his mind's eye, he could see poverty of Dickensian proportions, looming ahead. Three hundred and forty pounds was, after all, quite a small fortune. And there I left him.

"Go back to the shop lad and we'll bring the drill back later," said Twm, smiling benevolently. "He should never have brought you down here in the first place." I was tempted to tell him that I hadn't minded a bit, and was contemplating volunteering to work nights regular if each shift held such excitement. However, I said nothing.

I made my way back to the shop. The wind, if anything, had picked up, and the cold was intense. After the bright lights of the siding the darkness was, almost Stygian. Orion was beginning his descent down the western horizon. I wondered if he had witnessed the drama that had been played out and had shaken his head in bewilderment at the folly of Bryn Mawr?

---

* Bailiffs.

Picking up the Pieces

by

BRYAN DAVIES
(Ferndale)

'The art of music . . . is the expression of the soul of a nation'
(Ralph Vaughan Williams)

OR ANYONE seeking an insight into the musical identity of
the Welsh, perhaps the most obvious course of action would
be to spend a week at the National Eisteddfod. Within its
perimeter, Wales annually celebrates the cultural spectrum of a
people who have inhabited Britannia since pre-Christian times,
enjoying a hierocratic status significant enough to impress Roman
pragmatism.

Before the week is out, however, an astute observer would have
noticed that, whereas the literary branch of the festival can boast a
continuum dating back to the 6th century, the musical content
draws heavily on the products of other nations. Indeed, our
observer may well be prompted to ask, 'Is there not sufficient
Welsh music to furnish the various competitions and concerts?'
And the answer, quite simply, is – 'No'.

Many an ardent patriot has been stunned to discover that, to
date, only two manuscripts of ancient Welsh music have come to
light. The first is the ap Huw (c.1613), housed – ectopically – in
London [GB-LBI Add MS 14905]. Its preface states:

*'The following Manuscript is the Musick of the Britains, as settled
by a Congress, or Meeting of Masters of Music, by order of Gryffydd
ap Cynan, Prince of Wales, about A.D. 1100, with some of the*

most ancient pieces of the Britains, supposed to have been handed down to us from the British Druids.'

If this claim is true, then the arcane harp-tablature of the manuscript enshrines all that we have of the "genetically-unmodified" music of our ancestors.

The second manuscript is the so-called Penpont Antiphonal [NLWMS20541 E], a medieval missal containing the Office of St. David, which somehow escaped the purges of the English Reformation. So systemic, however, was Gregorian chant to the Norman Church that it hardly differs from other Offices of the time. Curiously enough, though, the hymn-tune 'Braint' bears a fleeting resemblance to one of its versicles – but this is probably quite accidental, a kind of Dorian double-take!

The 16th century Acts of Union so marginalized Wales that she had no hope of paralleling the great periods of music history which helped define European culture. There is no Welsh equivalent of Florence, Leipzig, Mannheim or Vienna; there is no pantheon dedicated to a Welsh Bach, Mozart, Beethoven and Wagner. Admittedly, genius appears when – and where – it will; but it can only flourish in a supportive environment. All the above-mentioned musical giants received a rigorous early education and were surrounded by the finest cultural models of the day. For Wales, until, effectively, the social reforms of the 20th century, it was a case of:

'Full many a flower is born to lush unseen
And waste its sweetness on the desert air'.

In the meantime, anyone with musical talent had to seek patronage of some kind or other. One such "indenture" was the post of domestic harper to a wealthy landowner. John Parry ('Parri Ddall') [?-1782], an early collector of folk tunes, was domestic harper to Sir Watcyn Williams Wynn, whose residence – Wynnstay – was occasionally visited by the great Mr. Handel. The outer movements of Parry's Harp Sonata in D demonstrate the extent of "Handel fever" but the melody of its central Andante is none other than – 'Dafydd y Garreg Wen'.

Even the legacy of the iconic Dr. Joseph Parry [1841-1903], when looked at realistically, lies more in its educational beneficence than through any universal appraisal of his music. For whatever reasons, Parry settled for the rather specious sentimentality of Victorian taste and never achieved the artistic heights of his European contemporaries.

Our hypothetical observer at the Eisteddfod would soon have gathered that, apart from the folk-music classes, most of the home-grown music was written in the 20th century. Wales, at long last, can display a relatively small, but growing corpus of music which can stand shoulder-to-shoulder with its counterparts in the rest of the world.

But does it manifest a distinctive Welsh identity? Well, some of it does. For example, Grace Williams's 'Penillion for orchestra', as its title suggests, is a synthesis of demonstrably Welsh musical characteristics. Mansel Thomas's setting of R. Williams Parry's 'Y Bardd' is acknowledged, by common consent, to be "the quintessential Welsh song". Close on its heels are songs by Meirion Williams, Dilys Elwyn Edwards and Eric Jones – exigencies of space alone preclude an exhaustive catalogue. For, according to Rousseau:

> *'It is the accent of languages that determines the melody of each nation'.*

One final speculation – and the rest is silence.

Can cultural identity possibly survive the relentless deluge of commercial dross – the latest, and perhaps the most destructive "invader"? Before a new Dark Age threatens finally to extinguish the light, maybe we should ponder the words of Dr. Maya Patel:

> *'The country that has abandoned its culture to commerce deserves a Coca Cola wake'.*

Welsh Identity without Illusion

by

BRIAN DAVIES
(Pontypridd)

S O WHAT SORT OF Welsh are we in the valleys? Firstly, a few personal comments. My father's family were Welsh-speaking. My grandfather came to Penrhiwceiber from Troedyrhiw as jobs moved from iron to coal. My grandmother was brought south from Blaenau Ffestiniog when quarrying families sought work on the coalfield. I vaguely recall her efforts to teach me some Welsh, with no success. My mother's family were half South Walian, half West Country. The South Walian side had mostly lost their Welsh in her generation. Her father had come to Mountain Ash from Wiltshire to find work as a haulier underground. I think this background makes me fairly typical of the mixed population of the valleys, although with some the English element in the family will be replaced or augmented by Irish, Spanish, Italian, or Polish, to list only the most obvious possibilities.

I went to Church services with my mother, and to Welsh Independent Chapel with my father. Chapel services were much better theatre, though I could follow very little of what the minister was saying. My parents sang in both languages in the mixed choir which practised and often performed in the chapel, and was conducted by my father's eldest brother who was also the chapel organist. My father's youngest brother sang in the same choir, and later became conductor of Ystradgynlais Male Voice. The fourth brother eventually became a deacon out of a sense of duty, although he had no religious beliefs. Three out of the four brothers either joined or supported the Communist Party for many years, while still attending chapel.

In school we were often taught Welsh by the teacher who was also responsible for religious instruction, making it seem that the one subject was a branch of the other; an association which had already formed in my mind because of chapel. We were of the generation of teenagers who, in other parts of Wales, were enthused by Gwynfor Evans' first election victory; but I can recall only one real convert in our class: the rest of us remained unconvinced, myself most definitely.

I first realised that I had better think through what it meant to be Welsh in spite of all these ambiguities when I went to university in York. There it soon became clear that my willingness to accept a British identity was shared only by Ulster Protestants. The English were English, and had no notion of a larger Britain, except for those of the teaching staff who had been in the armed forces during the war. But being Welsh in England also had its complications. A Welsh Society was formed at the university at this time but I wasn't invited to join, presumably because I was obviously ineligible. Never mind, I was in good company. If I remember correctly, Gwyn A. Williams, then Prof. of History before his return to Wales a few years later, and his wife Maria weren't invited either.

That was over thirty years ago, but the persistence in some quarters of the attitude that full membership of the nation is confined to the 20% or so who speak Welsh can be more than a cause of minor personal irritation.

I have to admit that ignorance of cultural reality in Wales is two-sided. When I was at school in the Cynon valley we did not know that Welsh-speaking Wales existed. The first time that I met people of my own age whose first language was Welsh was when I went to university at York and later Swansea. Many people in the valleys still have no personal experience of contact with Welsh-speaking communities. Quite a few do not believe that such communities exist, and regard Welsh-language policy as a trick by a middle-class clique to monopolise the best jobs in the public sector. The South-East, with the bulk of the population, sometimes has the feel of a cultural enclave, open to the English-speaking world but strangely distant from the rest of Wales.

On the other hand I still regularly meet people of all ages from West and North Wales whose version of Welsh history does not include any rational explanation of the existence of the English-speaking communities of the South-East. Sensible and educated people can still be heard explaining that the Welsh of Glamorgan and Gwent simply 'gave up' on the language, or that a punitive educational system using the 'Welsh Not' succeeded here while, for some unexplained reason, the same system failed totally in Gwynedd.

The reality of the situation is both easier to explain and more difficult to deal with. The use of the Welsh language declined in the valleys in proportion to the arrival of hundreds of thousands of people, mainly from England, sucked into the coalfield by the demand for labour. The town of Pontypridd is both an extreme example of this process and a cause for realistic optimism. When Evan and James James composed 'Mae Hen Wlad fy Nhadau' in 1856 Pontypridd was a small, largely Welsh-speaking town of about 5,000 people. Half a century later it was a rapidly growing industrial centre of over 40,000 people, a majority of whom were first-generation English immigrants. This was what really finished off the teaching of Welsh in the town's schools, and forced the changing of some street names to English so that the residents could pronounce their addresses. A century later Pontypridd is still an overwhelmingly English-speaking town, but over 25% of its primary-school children attend Welsh-medium schools. This can be explained partly by the persistent campaigning of parents who want this education for their children, and by the strengthening of this lobby as a result of the recent movement into the town of families from Welsh-speaking areas. But this new migration is not sufficient to explain such a large interest in Welsh-medium education in an overwhelmingly English-speaking town.

Another factor has been at work in Pontypridd, I believe. The town's first historian was Owen Morgan, 'Morien' (1836-1921), whose writings are only ever referred to by conformist academics in tones of condescension and ridicule. It is true that some of his work on druidism makes the bemused reader wonder just what Morien was 'on' at the time. But his writings are of a different order when he is dealing with events which took place in his own lifetime. He was a good journalist, an honest recorder of his own times, a decent historian of mediaeval Wales, and a highly speculative writer on antiquity. Most importantly, he was the first Welsh-speaker in Pontypridd to realise that if the new population of his home town was to learn anything of the history and culture of the country which they would make their home they would have to acquire this knowledge in English. Morien's own books are now long out-of-print, but he influenced later writers, and this tradition of writing in English about the history of the town and the history of Wales has helped an immigrant population to make itself at home, and has I believe helped to create a climate in which there is support for the Welsh language among people who have never spoken a word of it themselves.

The South Wales valleys now have the largest percentage of people calling themselves Welsh in any part of Wales. Most of these people are in fact of very mixed origin, but they have been here now for four generations or more and they have 'gone native'. Our cultural identity cannot be the same as that of people in largely Welsh-speaking areas which have not experienced the same kind of population movement. But both communities can find a lot in common if we learn to talk to each other.

Home is Where the Heart is

by

PHYLLIS WAGSTAFF

W HEN ATTENDING junior school, my family moved to a new home in a small mining community near Chesterfield in Derbyshire. This meant a new start in a little village school. The classes were smaller than I was accustomed. The building, not being very large, had two classes in one room with just a single teacher. (How many teachers today would tolerate such conditions?) Nevertheless, this worked quite well; one section studying maths, reading and writing essays, whilst the rest were instructed on other subjects. We received a very good education, with excellent results.

Our schooling was very cosmopolitan, with teachers from Scotland, Ireland and Wales and, of course, England. Mrs. Anderson, our Scottish teacher, taught us the story of Robbie Burns, who became Scotland's most famous poet.

For Burns night Mrs. Anderson had a haggis sent down from Scotland. One of the mothers cooked 'tatties' and 'neeps' (no school kitchen in those days.) We sang the traditional Scottish songs, accompanied by scratchy records, played on an old wind up gramophone. Mrs. Anderson solemnly addressed the haggis before plunging in the knife, this I still remember.

Mrs. O'Mally, our fiery tempered teacher from Ireland, was not so forthcoming in teaching us about her country – although she always celebrated her patron Saint by wearing a bunch of shamrock on St Patrick's Day.

Our English teacher was very good at making history and geography lessons come alive. Mr. Smithers was a tall well built young man with red hair. (How we girls swooned over him.) I don't remember him using the cane, but he had a booming voice, which made us shiver in our shoes.

Our headmaster from Wales, Mr. Roberts (Bobby behind his back), was always immaculately dressed. Usually a very placid man, but could also be a strict disciplinarian. To me Wales was a distant land where the women wore tall black hats and red flannel shawls. The reason I believed this was from post cards sent from friends and relatives on holiday, depicting these images. On my first visit to the country I was very disappointed to see women ordinarily dressed. Later in life, I was introduced to Welsh culture through a friend from Wales whose marriage brought her to live in England. A talented musician and singer that never tired of talking about her native country.

True to Welsh tradition, Mr. Roberts' passion was Welsh history and music – a talented organist and choir master at the local village church. (His influence was infectious for it inspired me to learn to play the piano.) Our school choir was well known throughout the county, winning major prizes at the musical festivals (similar to the Welsh Eisteddfodau).

Apart from the compulsory set pieces, our own choice was invariably a Welsh song. 'David of the White Rock', 'The Ashgrove' and 'Men of Harlech'. The one that stayed in my mind was 'Ar Hyd y Nos', with the Welsh words being taught to us parrot fashion. At the end of the St. David's Day celebrations we sang 'Land Of My Fathers', with great gusto. Oh, how I wish I could remember the words, for whenever I hear the Welsh version it takes me back to my school days . . . 'Happy times'!

Mr. Roberts' interest in the local church took our choir to church concerts, fetes and entertaining the senior citizens. I shall always remember him telling us a Welsh legend. How Prince Llewelyn, when hunting, left faithful hound Gelert to guard his beloved baby son. On his return the cradle was upturned in a corner and Gelert bounded towards him in greeting, whilst his mouth was dripping with blood. Shocked at the thought of his son being killed by Gelert, Llewelyn drew his sword and killed the dog. Then with a last mournful look Gelert licked his master's hand and died. A cry drew his attention to the cradle. The boy was alive! Then Llewelyn, in looking around, saw the dead body of a wolf. Gelert had saved the child. Grief stricken; Llewelyn buried Gelert and placed a memorial stone on his grave, which became to be known as 'Bedd Gelert'.

Oh, how I loved that story! During a recent visit to the memorial stone at Bedd Gelert, I had vivid memories of those happy school days when Mr. Roberts told us that remorseful tale.

We were also told about the exploits of Owen Glendower. How he returned to his native land after a stay in England, and eventually styled himself as the first 'Prince of Wales'.

My only incursions into Wales, as a child, were family holidays on the north coast, and remembering a strange language being spoken by the locals.

After many years, my son moved to live in South Wales; here I spent many happy visits. The mountains were not unlike the Peak District of my native Derbyshire, but on a larger scale. I loved the Swansea coastline, with Mumbles and the nearby Gower Peninsular. At home I missed all this, for I lived many miles from the sea.

Time passed as I grew older. In 1998 I had the opportunity to move permanently into Wales and live near my family. Already having made many good friends on my previous frequent visits, I joined the local Church, and soon settled down in the area. This prompted me to join a Welsh language class (my family already spoke limited Welsh). I will never master the language; but having learnt how to pronounce the words, thus enables me to join in the singing of Welsh hymns. I really don't know all I am singing about, but I do recognise the tunes. This takes me back to my school days, for I see the face of Mr. Roberts all around me, and distinctively hear his fine tenor voice.

When in Wales I refer to Derbyshire as 'home', whilst there I speak of Wales as 'home', and can't wait to get back to my beloved mountains.

Mr. Roberts retired and returned to the land of his birth, of which he was very proud. I am sure it was this that helped me to settle down when I eventually came to live in Wales. I have been made to feel part of the community; enjoying visits to local Eisteddfodau, and participating in the St David's' Day celebrations.

Thank you Mr. Roberts for nurturing my interest in Wales!

An Epynt Shepherd

by

ANNETTE THOMAS

W HAT DOES IT mean to be Welsh? There is, of course, no definite answer for it means many things to different people. I would, however, like to offer my view on the subject through discussing someone I once knew. He was someone who was as Welsh as the valleys and mountains of Wales, but who also considered himself a citizen of the world. This person was my maternal grandfather.

Since he was a young lad my grandfather had been a shepherd on the Epynt where nearly everyone was related. Eventually he and his young family were forced out of this idyllic area to a nearby village, where the Council found work for him as a roadman. He revered the patch where he worked, through giving it the same loving care he had formerly given to his sheep. Leisure time to him was helping my father on our farm; gardening, shooting, fishing (often illegally), or anything else that needed doing. It could be said that my grandfather was a man of many parts, for he was a Parish Councillor and a deacon at the local chapel. He was nearing retirement age by the time I remembered him, and his children had grown up.

Yes, I was also born and brought up in this enchanting area of Wales. It is a tiny, scattered, rural community skirting the Epynt hillside. Those hills had been cleared of their people by the time I was born, to make way for an army training range preceding the Second World War, and absorbed into the nearest communities. Yet, the hearts and souls of that old Welsh stock of people still belong to those wide, bare slopes of Brycheiniog. Here you could hear the sound of silence amongst secret wooded dingles. Today this once peaceful tranquillity is disturbed by the firing of many military guns.

I had numerous other relatives living within walking distance, but it was with my grandparents that I spent most of my time. It is only now years later that I realise how much I have been influenced by them, especially my grandfather, as I followed his footsteps over the Epynt. It was from him and my mother – to whom he had passed his skills – that I learned about the countryside we lived in. He knew every stone and tree and how it all worked together. Each living thing had its place and a purpose, whilst the Epynt for miles around was as familiar to him as his own garden. The farmers, like my grandfather, who lived on the surrounding mountains, knew of all the sheep walks that existed there. I shall always remember the diligent manner my grandfather cared for his flock. During those days of 'bowed head in driving rain' he would tramp over the mountain to gather the sheep and shepherd them to safety, whilst measuring the ground to the rhythm of his steps. Oh, how well he knew that mountain!

The Epynt fog can happen suddenly and be both frightening and confusing out in those open spaces. "Don't be scared," he reassured me when this happened to us once, "that thorn tree over there on top of a bank leads to a dingle; there's a stream rising in the dingle which leads to the river". I had not been that way before, but sure enough we came safely to the river and a long walk home. He could tell you what the weather would do from the way the crows came home to roost, through explaining that a storm was imminent because the sheep were heading in a certain direction. He would also know when it would snow and when it was safe to cut the hay.

The knowledge that I have acquired of country lore has been entirely due to him. No books could have taught me so much. I learned in his company how to observe and study nature. Even today I still find myself calling fieldfares 'storm birds', wood pigeons 'quists', chaffinches 'twinks' and herons 'cranes'. He taught me how to track in the snow. I remember once, whilst we were shepherding in a February snowstorm, that he suddenly fell from my side onto a gorse bush. Thinking he had had a heart attack I leapt to his assistance. He got up, beaming, holding onto an unfortunate rabbit which he despatched with one swift chop of his hand. "Tracked him in," he said with satisfaction, "didn't come out."

He had passed on his skills as a shepherd to my mother. I listened to them with awe as they discussed their art, knowing each sheep as an individual – no mean feat in a flock of 700 – and followed them as faithfully as their dogs.

It was with my grandparents that I went to the little Chapel on the mountainside where I still worship, and where today I tend their grave. I recollect how proudly he sat in the big seat at the bottom of the pulpit, starting the hymn singing and taking around the elements of communion and the collection plate. It was to them that the preacher came to tea. I always felt it was a privilege to help my grandmother to set out the best china on the tea-table, prepare the best linen and enjoy her scrumptious cooking. The greatest satisfaction of all was listening to their after tea conversation when I was encouraged to participate. There was nothing small in those conversations, for they were all avid newspaper readers and listened to every scrap of news they could find on the radio. Thus, they had picked up a fair knowledge about many subjects, and, of course, had an opinion on everything.

My family had a wonderful sense of the ridiculous, finding something funny in almost every situation. Pompous people were a gift to my grandfather. He would encourage them to expound their views, whilst nodding gravely and throwing knowing looks at me and grandmother. Then they would go too far and offend his socialist soul. The resulting outburst was not pretty, but quickly over and forgotten. He was rarely deeply offended, but if very hurt, he was implacable in his future disdain. To his family, however, he was always supportive and full of pride in our achievements.

The greatest gift he bestowed on me personally was a sense of 'who I am'. "Remember," he said, fixing a bright blue and twinkling eye upon me, "you're no better than anyone else." Then, with a smile, he would continue: "Mind you, no-one else is any better than you are." I have tried to live by that advice, for it is the single most important thing I know. It has enabled me to meet everyone on equal terms and to value everyone equally.

I could write far more about him; his story telling; his immaculate garden; the walking sticks he made in winter; teaching me to tickle trout on warm summer's evenings; laughing at himself when something went wrong; above all his countryman's wisdom and immense rustic dignity. He was one of the pillars of our community. Chapel events, singing in a choir, attending graziers' meetings and travelling around the villages to enjoy sporting activities were all very much part of my grandfather's Epynt life. He was, as to be expected, one of the founders of our local eisteddfod which still thrives.

I have followed my grandfather as a Parish Councillor, Chapel Elder and, since the age of fourteen, I have been Treasurer of our eisteddfod. I am proud to have been able to contribute to the continuity of life in this small corner of Wales. Through this journey, as through the days we spent together, my grandfather's Welsh spirit has been my constant companion.

In my Soul I am Welsh

by

MAGGIE WAGSTAFF

A place of birth has nothing to do with an identity

LONG BEFORE I was born Granma and Grandfather bought a smallholding deep in the depths of a large wood. The land, around thirteen acres apart from a clearing of about three, was covered in trees. I shall always remember that isolated hamlet in Derbyshire, which was Paradise for a child!

My maternal granma's family totalled six children, and Mam, the youngest, was only eight years old when her father died. As the family grew older, each in turn married and bought small plots of land nearby, setting up smallholdings themselves. They all had families of their own, so my coming to this world was idyllic, with me being cosseted and spoilt.

"Your grandfather was a Welshman, and could sing like an angel," Granma told me, "his tenor voice, so rich, it was a pleasure to hear. He was in a male voice choir, you know, and competed in the Welsh Eisteddfodau." I listened intently to her talking about my grandfather and his strong personality. She also told me of Merlin the wizard; of dragons that flew and lived in caves and then I would pester her for more stories.

"Where is Welsh, Granma?" I asked tugging at her skirt to wake her from her dreams . . .

"Eh . . . a long way in the mountains." She grunted and, chin on her chest, resumed her nap. My imagination ran riot. I pictured caves in the rocks with huge giants; dragons belching fire and flying far over the mountaintops.

Granma still kept grandfather's music, and would listen intently to any Welsh music on the radio. Her secret ambition was for one of us to follow in his footsteps and become either a great singer or a musician. Auntie Dru was Mam's older sister and married to Uncle Ted. They lived next door, across the field, so it was easy access even for the smallest of children. As always, I was staying with her whilst Mam was shopping in the town. This was a marathon jaunt, one and a half miles to walk to the bus and then a further hour journey to the town. This she did every week, laden with heavy shopping bags, mostly uphill on the way home. Always she would pass *that* grim-looking school building, where they kept lots of children behind dark brick walls and closed gates.

"But, Mam, I don't want to go home yet!" I protested as I hid and peeped out from under Auntie's pleated skirt. "I like it here; I've not eaten my ice-cream!" This was auntie's special homemade custard from her own recipe that I called 'ice-cream'.

"Come now, go and fetch the dress we made for your doll and take it home with you," Auntie coaxed. "Your dolly will like that." There were very few harsh words spoken and yet she had a matter of fact way of getting things done.

"Okay, but I'll bring dolly with me next time," was my just as cunning answer, for maybe then I could stay the night?

I loved staying there and was drawn to her like a moth to a flame. She would spoil me with cakes and her homemade 'ice-cream', and sit and tell me wonderful stories of princesses rescued from monsters; and of fairy folk playing harps in far-off Wales. Although she was only five feet tall, to me she appeared large in stature, and I could curl cosily on her lap and go to sleep. Her hair, as long as I knew, was silver white and lay in soft curls around her homely face, which was always full of smiles.

It was on one of these Saturdays that I had been allowed to stay the night. Uncle Ted was working the night shift so I'd kept Auntie company in her big soft comfy bed. My cousin Aline was home from College for the weekend. It was one of those sleepy summer days when everyone just stays idle.

"Come on you," said my Auntie, "let's have a cuddle." Then

she would lift me on to her knee with a squeeze so hard that I was buried in the folds of her apron. She always wore an apron over her frock, but it was an overall type apron without sleeves. It gave the effect of her having layers of skirts, which was an ideal place for hiding under as it was like an immense tent. On the front was a large pocket, which was a favourite hiding place for many things, including a large hankie bigger than a tablecloth. With this she was forever cleaning my face. "You are a mucky pup," and then from deep inside those layers she would produce a boiled sweet that lasted for hours . . . Magic! After a story, I was put into the large white stone sink in the kitchen, and given a bath. "It's no use squirming; the muck's got to come off." And the rough flannel scraped my neck and face to a bright shade of pink, after which I was dressed tidy, and left to sulk.

Then everyone was thumb-twiddling, and heel-kicking, not knowing what to do, when Auntie came up with a great idea, or so it seemed at the time!

"Come on, we will fill the large basket with goodies and go to the wood for the afternoon and look for those dragons." No sooner said than she busied herself organising food and drinks for all. Sandwiches, cakes and all sorts of goodies, blackberry and apple pie, flasks of tea and my favourite dragon's blood (raspberryade), were all placed in the basket covered with a large tablecloth. "We had better have a couple of blankets to sit on – oh – I think we had better have the wheelbarrow too – don't you?" She laughed.

With enough rations for an army, we set out down through the garden heading for the field beyond. Auntie carried the basket of food, Aline had the blankets on which to sit and I carried a large towel.

Auntie sang out with a fine voice, "Count your blessings one by one . . ." and I tried to join in by la-lahing the words. "You need your grandfather round you, young lady, he could really sing," she said. "His strong Welsh voice would have echoed around these trees. You would have loved your grandfather . . . He will be singing with the angels now."

Across the field and into the wood, we wound our way, following the path to the brook and a small pond dammed by a bridge. I imagined the squirrels to be red dragons flying through the trees and breathing fire at the bushes. We crossed over and set everything down on the bank. Auntie put one of the blankets down on the ground for the food and the other for us to sit on. Everyone sat around tucking into the goodies that lay out before us, drank tea from the multicoloured picnic mugs, and lazed in the shade by the pond side.

"I'm going to look for baby dragons!" I yelled, and headed sharply towards the pond.

"Come away from the water," Aline shouted and made a lunge to grab my arm. Being small I ducked. I ran and hid behind the nearest tree, only to hear an almighty splash and see water cascading everywhere. I was not the flavour of the month. "Wait 'til I catch you!" came the screams from the water. "You and your damned dragons!" Aline emerged from the pond dripping; covered in green slime and mud and looking very disgruntled.

"You didn't have to go in to find the dragons," laughed Auntie, and handed Aline the towel.

I was given a strong dressing down from Auntie and some very dirty looks from Aline as she tried to dry off.

"Good job I carried the towel isn't it!" I grinned. "Can I have a paddle in the brook now?" This remark could not have gone very well, because I was urged home briskly by Auntie. "It's not fair! Aline had a paddle," I grumped, ". . . and I carried the towel!"

"Just like your grandfather, always had an answer and stubborn 'til the end . . . never knew when to let it be," came Auntie's reply. I shrugged my shoulders and stormed in the direction of home.

"Wait 'til you start school," my cousin called after me. "You just wait; then you'll have to behave!"

The woodland was my security, my world, and beyond this I knew little other than the stories my family related. The trees enveloped my small frame and gave me a safe warm feeling that I never questioned. My enquiring mind grew in a tranquil loving environment shielded from the reality of life beyond.

Woken early by my mam's insistence one dark Monday morning, I was dressed in my best clothes, and my long curls were plaited and tied with plain white ribbons.

"Where are we going?" I insisted – quite excited by the fact that I was going with Mam, and not to be left with Auntie.

"You are going to school!" Mam replied cautiously, and I could sense anguish in her voice. "There will be lots of other children and you will have books to read." She knew my love of books and even at the age of four I had been taught to read by my cousin, who was a teacher.

Swallowing hard I tried to reply, but the excitement and the fear held my voice tight, and the words stuck in my throat. I had heard about school and had passed the place once – viewing the children through the large iron gates that barred their exit.

Leaving my sister with Granma, Mam took hold of my hand, and together we walked quietly along the dusty cart track leading to the village. My heart was pounding and I did not feel like running; Mam's grip on my hand tightened when we neared those cold high grey school walls.

"You'll be alright now!" she said, trying to reassure us both as we passed through those ominous black gates. There, we were confronted by other girls and boys, tightly clutching and clinging to their mams. How I wished I was going to the wood for a picnic with Auntie.

"I've never seen so many children," I said, "do they all live here?"

A rather large lady appeared from inside the building and beckoned everyone to go in. Swallowing hard I clung to Mam's little finger like the last leaf on the tree, knowing I had to let go, but holding fast to that last moment when the lady – like the wind – tore me away.

"Come now child, leave your coat on a peg in the cloakroom and then go into that classroom there," she said.

Turning round I found Mam had vanished, I couldn't run after her as I was still caught in the grip of the rather large lady. For the first time in my life I felt so lost and alone, even though other children surrounded me.

"Yo' one o' them Woodite's," came this voice from behind, "tha' don't belong 'ere." And this rough looking boy with dark hair and holey trousers prodded me sharply. "Get back t' wood w'ere thar came from."

I didn't understand what he meant, but sensed his hostility. What had I done to provoke him? Suddenly I felt that this was an alien place where I did not belong, and that I was like a foreigner in a strange land. Aline could dress me down as much as she liked, if she would only fetch me away from this place. Then my Auntie's words came to me in the song she would sing to me in the wood, 'Count your blessings one by one'. That determination I had inherited from my grandfather welled up inside me. I brushed away the tears that stung my eyes, and swallowed hard.

"I don't understand a word you are saying, and I don't like you, so go away and boil your head!" I shouted at the boy, "and I hope the dragons get you."

Head high, I walked into the classroom feeling much better, even if I thought I didn't belong there . . . and yet, I did – or was it somewhere else? Then I had a strange feeling and thought of my grandfather and how proud he was to be a Welshman. One day I shall follow his footsteps to that place they call Wales. During that precise moment I felt in my heart, mind and soul, that I was Welsh.

gymuned; ac mae hynny'n
gwacáu'r llwyfannau a fu.

Yma nawr, mae'i amen o'n
galw ym mhob un galon
am barhâd i'w ganiadau
yn eco hir llenni'n cau;
am denor i'w hagor nhw,
â'n hunawdydd yn lludw.

I neuaddau'n llonyddu,
down â'n dawn yn nodau du;
down o hyd i'w donau o
yn y gweryd, a'u geirio;
down â'n hunawd i'n heniaith,
a rhoi'r gainc Gymraeg i'r gwaith.

I Dŷ Coch, cawn godi cân
o enaid Wmffra'i hunan;
i'r Betws dywedwst, daw
eilwaith ddesgant ei alaw;
a draw, draw o sŵn y stryd,
emynau i'r Waun bob munud!

*   *   *

Y mae'r düwch mor dawel
ag aria ola'i ffarwél,
a heno, mae caneuon
yn rhad, mor ofer â hon.
Ei diwn ef, nid â'n ofer,
â'n nos hyll mor brin o sêr.

Karen Owen

Murddun

Ni weli, Gymro, wrth it grwydro'r fro
Y murddun hwn dan ddrain a'i furiau'n chwâl,
Ni eilw'r hynafieithydd yn ei dro
I chwilio'r sail â thrywel neu a phâl;
Ac ofer holi gwybodusion llên
A anwyd yma lenor mawr neu fardd,
Can's nid o feini nac o feini hen
Y creuwyd caer ein hiaith doreithiog, hardd.
Ei deunydd hi oedd geiriau bychan, rhad,
A myrdd o ddywediadau ffraeth a chu
Oedd fwrlwm ar leferydd mam a thad,
A hiwmor 'tir glas, tir coch, tir du'.
Mae'r adeiladwyr hoff ym mhridd y llan
A chwalwyr hyf, estronaidd ym mhob man.

J. Beynon Phyllips

Y Gymraes Newydd

Caeodd Seisnigrwydd
y drws yn glep,
a'i gadael, fy nghariadferch,
yn brae i lygaid barus
y nos.

Manteisiodd
Uchelgais, Hunan lesâd,
Elw a Snobyddiaeth
ar ei swildod
a'i thrin fel un
'ohonyn nhw'
i'w gwthio o'r palmant.

Heddiw,
       fe'i gwelais
ar rodfa ffasiwn
yn hardd a thrwsiadus
yn deffro cynnwrf.

J. Beynon Phyllips

Amgueddfa Werin Cymru

Gwrandewch
ar eiriau
plwyfolion y gorffennol
yn atsain eu cennad
o stiwdio glywedog y cof.

Clustfeiniwch
am sylwadau pigog cydwybod, a chlywed iaith
hen werin anweledig Sain Ffagan
yn drwgdybio
dyfodol
ein hunaniaeth Gymreig.

Teimlwch gryndod trai amser
yn llusgo
ei neges grafog
   yn ôl
     i ddwnsiwn llwyd
        yr ymennydd.
Gwrandewch!

A fedrwch glywed eneidiau
yr hen frethyn cartre'
yn wylofain
rhwng meini'r muriau?

Synhwyrwch gri eu harswyd
yn lletya
yn nistawrwydd anesmwyth
Sain Ffagan.

Gwrandewch
ar rwgnach yr ymadawedig
wrth grynhoi
yn anadl o leisiau atgofus
dan nenfwd to gwellt
   Nant Wallter.

A fedrwch glywed
rhai o werinwyr anghofiedig
yr echdoe
yn datgan eu barn
yn efail Llawr-y-glyn?

Gwrandewch ar eu llef
yn hollti'r tawelwch
rhwng curiadau cyson
   y pedoli.
A fedrwch synhwyro
achwyniadau
hen hoelion wyth Sain Ffagan
yn mynegi eu barn
ar fainc rheithgor
yr isymwybod
   ein bod yn euog
   o ddiystyru Cymreictod
   ein hachau
   diwylliedig
   trwy fabwysiadu
      difaterwch gwag ein byd?

A fedrwch annog eich dychymyg
i glywed
achwyniadau trigolion
y cynefinoedd gwerinol, cyn gweld eu hwynebau
yn toddi
   i liw llwyd
    y meini?

A tybed
pa un o ysbrydion Beca
fydd yn herio
eneidiau clwc y dyfodol
trwy ddod allan o feini
      Tolldu Penparcau
             â phicell yn ei law?

Pwy
o blith y genhedlaeth newydd
fydd yn gwresogi'r meini
â thân
emynau Pantycelyn
yng nghapel Pen-rhiw,
neu
a fydd dieithrwch eu cainc
      yn tagu'r geiriau?

Yfory
pa Gymro
a dagrau yn ei lygaid
fydd yn cylchdroi'n hiraethus
o amgylch
muriau anghofiedig y werin, gan lusgo ei ddwylo
yn annwyl
dros wyneb llychlyd
      y meini?

Cefnfab

Very Welsh

gan

EUROS JONES EVANS

NID DISGRIFIAD O ddarn o gig eidion un o wartheg duon Cymru ar gownter gwaedlyd mewn siop gigydd mohono; nid label ar olwythion cig oen o lethrau'r Preseli ydoedd, nac ychwaith sylw gan feirniad mewn het fowler wrth graffu'n fanwl ar gobyn Cymreig llamsachus yn arddangos ei gyhyrau sgleiniog ynghanol cylch y Royal Welsh. Na, dyfarniad meddyg coleg o gyflwr fy iechyd i ydoedd; canlyniad archwiliad meddygol pan oeddwn yn lasfyfyriwr. *Very Welsh*. Dau air a gofnodwyd yn ddiseremoni frysiog mewn blwch ar ffurflen iechyd swyddogol Coleg Prifysgol Cymru Abertawe; dau air a gadarnhaodd yr hyn a ofnaswn ers rhai blynyddoedd, sef bod rhyw feirws yn fy ngwythiennau a barai i ryw gloffni swil ddod drosof bob tro y byddwn yn agor fy ngheg i lefaru neu'n hytrach i seinio'r iaith fain.

A minnau bellach, ddeugain mlynedd wedyn, yn cael amser i adfyfyrio ar y profiadau hynny a wnaeth 'fy ngreddf yn lleddf a llon', rhaid cydnabod na ches i byth wared â'r feirws hwnnw a gafodd ei ddiagnosio mor annisgwyl pan oeddwn yn ddeunaw oed. Y mae'n eitha posibl mai dyna a fu'n gyfrifol am lywio fy rhawd mewn gwirionedd ac a achosodd imi benderfynu yn gymharol ifanc mai gwasanaethu'r Gymraeg y byddwn yn ei wneud gydol fy mywyd. Yn awr ac yn y man, pan fydd haint yn blino dyn ac anifail gan fygwth cymdeithas gyfan, y cam cyntaf i'w ddileu yw ceisio olrhain ei darddiad. Wrth fynd ar drywydd y feirws 'Cymreictod' hwn a fu'n rhan mor annileadwy ohonof, yr wyf yn berffaith siŵr mai ymhlith pobl a thir plwyf Cilymaenllwyd yng nghornel isaf Sir Gâr y gafaelodd ynof gyntaf. Yno roedd y Gymraeg yn endemig.

Gan fod tipyn o ddadlau wedi bod yn ddiweddar gan ieith-addysgwyr ynglŷn â pha un sydd bwysicaf: caffael iaith ynteu dysgu iaith, y mae'n rhaid imi gyfaddef mai'r dylanwadau ieithyddol naturiol o'n cwmpas sydd fwyaf llwyddiannus. Diau mai felly y bu yn fy hanes. Roedd y teulu yn nyth o Gymreictod: fy nhad yn hanu o Geredigion a mam yn un o rocesi prydferthaf a fagodd sir Benfro, ynghyd â'm tri brawd hŷn, Dafydd, Geraint ac Iestyn. Cymraeg oedd iaith chwarae ffwtbol, iaith chwarae cowbois, iaith pysgota, a iaith cwmpo mas. Annedd y mans ydoedd a diau bod yr enw Llys-myfyr a roddwyd arno yn awgrymog iawn. Dyna sicrhau amgylch-fyd o lyfrau aneirif, trafodaethau diwinyddol a sŵn pregeth yn cael ei pharatoi o fewn clyw yn wythnosol. Byddai ein byd yn troi o gwmpas Capel Calfaria, Login. Bob Sul caem gyfle i wrando ar iaith safonol y pulpud tra byddai iaith William Morgan yn cael ei roi ar gof a chadw trwy ddysgu adnodau a pharatoi ar gyfer y Gymanfa Bwnc flynyddol.

Yn y Gymraeg y byddem yn chwedleua â'n gilydd: pob ffrind a chymydog; mewn gwirionedd pawb yn yr ardal, heblaw am un. Y bwtsiwr o Hendy-gwyn oedd hwnnw a ddeuai'n rheolaidd yn ei ffedog o streipiau glas a gwyn i'n tŷ bob nos Wener. Gan mai monoglot o Sais oedd hwn, cawn dipyn o hwyl yn ceisio cyfathrebu ag ef yn ei iaith ei hun. Nid Saes di-Gymraeg mohono ond gŵr a barablai'n llafarog lithrig ac a gyferbynnai'n fawr a'm hymdrechion geirfaol anhyblyg i a ymdebygai i anystwythder a gwytnwch y cig maharen a oedd wedi'i lapio dan ei liain hambwrdd staenedig. Mewn gwirionedd, rhywbeth dieithr ac estron oedd Saesneg i ni; tresmaswr a sangai ar gytgord ein Cymreictod. Cyfnod dideledu ydoedd, a'r weiarles (pan nad oedd y batri asid yn fflat) oedd y falf unffordd a adawai lif yr iaith anghyfarwydd i mewn i'n cartref yn awr ac yn y man. Does dim syndod mai nefoedd i'n clyw oedd gwrando ar raglenni Cymraeg prin megis Oedfa'r Bore, a Chaniad-aeth y Cysegr ar y Suliau, Raligamps ar nos Sadwrn ac, yn uchaf-bwynt ar y cwbl, SOS Galw Gari Tryfan ar nos Fawrth.

Ac yn yr ysgol fach – Ysgol Ffynnon-wen – mi gaem wersi hanes, daearyddiaeth, syms, ac ambell i wers fach, ie, ambell i wers fach o English yn Gymraeg chwarae teg am mai Cymry bach oeddem ni.

Bob dydd Gwener aem ati i ddysgu barddoniaeth: barddoniaeth Gymraeg ac English poetry bob yn ail wythnos. Ysgrifennwyd y cerddi mewn llawysgrifen firain ar y bwrdd du a safai ar bedeircoes lych-lyd yng nghornel y rŵm mowr. Ni wnaed llawer o ymgais i egluro'r penillion. Y dasg ddiflas yn ddieithriad oedd eu dysgu ar ein cof. Y cyntaf i gyflawni hynny a gâi ganiatâd i fynd adref yn gynnar. Er nad yw'r cof cystal bellach, fe weithiai'n ddi-baid am rai oriau yn ystod y dyddiau Gwener hynny. Y canlyniad oedd fy mod yn fynych yn cael ffoi yn gynnar oddi wrth ddesg a bwrdd du.

Yna, un diwrnod, fe'i cofiaf fel ddoe, daeth cnoc ar ddrws yr ysgol. Pwy safai yno ond dynes osgeiddig hardd mewn cot werdd dywyll, het uchel o'r un lliw ac yn gwisgo sbecol swyddogol. Cyflwynodd ei hunan fel Miss Margaret Jenkins, A.E.M. – un o Arolygwyr ei Mawrhydi. Yn gwrtais iawn gofynnodd am gael siarad â'r dosbarth i gyd. Fe'n holodd ynglŷn â chestyll Cymru a gofynnodd a oeddem wedi gweld llun o gastell Harlech o gwbl. Mentrais godi llaw a dweud: 'Do Miss, ar nymbar eighteen Typhoo Tea.' Chwarddodd yn iach gan ddiolch yn ddistaw bach efallai fod yr holl gardiau arwyr, adar, ceir, awyrennau a chestyll a gasglem fel plant oddi ar becynnau bwyd a phacedi sigarets yn gyfryngau addysgol mor anuniongyrchol ddylanwadol. Ond yna, mewn llais addfwyn iawn, adroddodd bennill syml iawn wrthym:

> Hen hosan a'i choes yn eisie – ei brig
> Heb erioed ei ddechre;
> Ei throed heb bwyth o'r ede,
> Hynny yw dim, onid de?

Holodd ac esboniodd. Dyma'r tro cyntaf imi erioed glywed am englyn a chynghanedd. Rhoes hanes Gwydderig a Brynaman inni ac ymhen rhyw hanner awr fe'm cyfareddwyd gan y wybodaeth. Yn yr ychydig funudau hynny agorwyd byd newydd a daear newydd. Cliciodd rhywbeth yn nyfnder fy mod. Roedd gan y Gymraeg rywbeth gwerthfawr i'w gynnig. Yn gyflym ymgartrefodd y feirws o'm mewn. Nid oeddwn ond deg oed ar y pryd.

Yn rhinwedd fy swydd wrth hyfforddi athrawon crybwyllais yn

gyson mai dim ond unwaith y mae plentyn yn ddeg oed. Gan fod perthnasedd yn un o egwyddorion pwysig y Cwricwlwm Cenedlaethol, dylid sicrhau ei fod yn cael y cyfleoedd sy'n gweddu i'r oed hwnnw. Ond, wedi dweud hynny, y mae yr un mor bwysig ei fod yn cael profiadau sydd yn ymestyn y tu hwnt i ffiniau dosbarth a'i fod yn cael ei gyflwyno yn awr ac yn y man i brofiadau'r byd mawr. Yr oedd cynnal lecsiwn yn achlysur cymdeithasol tra phwysig bryd hynny. Defnyddid ein hysgol i gynnal cyfarfodydd gwleidyddol. Yn nechrau 1957, pan fu farw Syr Rhys Hopkin Morris, Aelod Seneddol Caerfyrddin, cynhaliwyd isetholiad. Yr oeddwn wedi clywed fy nhad yn sôn llawer bod dynes ifanc eithriadol yn sefyll dros Blaid Cymru. Dyma'r tro cyntaf imi ymgyfarwyddo ag enw'r blaid honno hefyd. Yn ei Awstin Ten 1938 aeth o gwmpas yr ardal yn annog pawb i ddod i wrando arni yn Ysgol Ffynnon-wen. Ac felly y bu. Llanwyd y lle. Yna fe gyrhaeddodd y ddynes ifanc hon, Jennie Eirian Davies, yng nghwmni gŵr bonheddig iawn yr olwg. Ie, Gwynfor Evans ei hunan. Nid ymffrost mo hyn ond gallaf dystio, er mor ifanc oeddwn, imi gael fy ngwefreiddio gan areithiau y ddau. Mae'n rhaid imi gyfaddef nad oeddwn yn deall llawer iawn ond roedd rhyw angerdd a didwylledd anghyffredin yn y traethu; y math o draethu argyhoeddedig a dreiddia i ddyfnder bodolaeth dyn. Yr argraff fawr a gefais gan y ddau oedd bod Cymru a'r iaith Gymraeg yn bwysig a bod yn rhaid ymdrechu i wneud popeth i'w diogelu. Y noson honno gwreiddiodd y feirws ynof.

Dyddiau yr Eleven Plus oedd y rheiny. Er nad oeddwn wedi cyrraedd yr oed priodol, fe'm cynghorwyd i'w sefyll flwyddyn ymlaen llaw er mwyn cael 'profiad' o'r arholiad. O'r herwydd ychydig iawn o baratoi a fu gan nad oedd disgwyl imi basio. Daeth y diwrnod mawr. Dal y bws i Ysgol Ramadeg Hendy-gwyn. Cael cryn hwyl ar y papurau i gyd heblaw am yr adran Saesneg. Gadael y cwestiwn allan. Nid oeddwn yn ei ddeall!

Ac yna digwyddodd rhywbeth rhwng sefyll yr arholiad a chael y canlyniad a fu'n drobwynt yn fy mywyd. Cafodd fy nhad alwad i weinidogaethu yn y Ponciau, ger Wrecsam. Er mawr loes, gwawriodd diwrnod y symud, diwrnod y ffarwelio a diwrnod y tynnu gwreiddyn a'i drawsblannu mewn daear anghydnaws. Bellach yn lle rhyddid cae, fferm ac afon, caethiwed strydoedd, tai coch a phyllau glo; yn lle persawredd silwair, gwair a dom da, gorfod dioddef arogleuon cemegol Monsanto ac, yn lle cynhesrwydd cartrefol ysgol fach wledig, oerni niwtral ac amhersonol ysgol fawr Seisnig.

Yn ystod y dyddiau di-hwyl a di-wên hynny pan oedd hiraeth yn feunyddiol yn llwydo gorwelion maboed, daeth telegram bach melyn yn fy hysbysu fy mod, er mawr syndod i bawb, wedi pasio'r Eleven Plus. Yna, ym mis Medi 1957, dyma Iestyn, fy mrawd, a minnau'n dechrau yn Ysgol Ramadeg y Bechgyn Rhiwabon. Canfod yn syth mai Seisnig oedd ethos yr ysgol er bod tipyn o gydymdeimlad yno tuag at y Gymraeg. Emynau Saesneg yn y bore ac ambell i emyn Cymraeg yn awr ac yn y man. Ond i ddod yn ôl at y gwersi. Saesneg oedd y cyfan heblaw am y Gymraeg ac Ysgrythur. Canfod yn fuan fy anallu i ysgrifennu'n rhugl a chywir yn yr iaith anghyfarwydd honno. Sylwadau yr athro Saesneg yn ddieithriad ar ddiwedd fy ymdrechion traethodol oedd: Good content but still too much Welsh in it! Ymdrechu i ddeall llenyddiaeth yr iaith fain, a gwawd yn aml gan sawl bwli yn y dosbarth oherwydd fy acen Gymraeg. Camynganu geiriau wrth geisio darllen rhai llinellau o ddramâu y bardd o Stratford. A minnau o'r herwydd yn destun sbort, a dirmyg. Ffeit yn dilyn ac o dan bob clais ar fraich ac wyneb, dyfnhaodd y feirws ynof.

Y canlyniad oedd bod y Gymraeg yn awr yn rhywbeth mwy na phwnc imi. Gwefr oedd cael gafael ar unrhywbeth a oedd wedi'i ysgrifennu yn yr iaith. Yn ffodus ymaelododd fy nhad yn llyfrgell gyhoeddus Wrecsam. Dilynwn ef yno'n wythnosol gan fod yno gornel wedi'i neilltuo i lyfrau Cymraeg. Heb fod yn ymffrostgar, darllenais bob llyfr yn yr adran honno erbyn imi gyrraedd tair ar ddeg oed. Cael cyfle i ymelwa ar lenyddiaeth anturiaethus nofelwyr megis E. Morgan Humphreys, Meuryn, John Ellis Williams, R. Bryn Williams a T. Llew Jones gan enwi ond ychydig. Amheuthun oedd blasu iaith rywiog raenus a nodweddai'r awduron hyn i gyd. Suddodd teithi'r iaith i'm personoliaeth. Bu'r cyfan yn wrtaith i'r feirws.

Yn yr ysgol braint oedd cael cyfle i fod wrth draed sawl Gamaliel o athro Cymraeg: Degwel Owen, dramodydd a darlithydd; Cyril

Hughes, awdur *Catrin o Ferain*, ynghyd â'r prifeirdd Geraint Bowen a Bryan Martin Davies. Ond er mor ddylanwadaol y gall athrawon ysgol fod, rhaid sôn am un profiad allgyrsiol allweddol a lywiodd fy awydd i fod yn athro Cymraeg. Un nos Sul cyhoeddwyd o'r sedd fawr yn ein capel fod y Prifardd Euros Bowen, yn cynnal dosbarth dysgu'r gynghanedd yn Ysgol Y Grango, Rhos, o dan nawdd y W.E.A. Pedair ar ddeg oeddwn ar y pryd a chan nad oedd arholiadau tyngedfennol am ryw ddwy flynedd arall penderfynais ymuno â'r dosbarth. Diau bod yr hedyn cynganeddol a heuwyd ynof rai blynyddoedd ynghynt gan yr HMI yn Ysgol Ffynnon-wen yno o hyd ond ei fod mewn hunedd. Ond fe'i deffrowyd gan Euros ac ymhen rhai misoedd gallwn gynganeddu'n rhwydd iawn. Yn raddol datblygodd y ddawn i lunio cwpled, yna englyn a chywydd. Ymhen y flwyddyn dyma benderfynu ymgeisio am gadair yn eisteddfod flynyddol ysgol Rhiwabon. Bûm wrthi am bron i dri mis yn ysgrifennu awdl ar y testun Yr Arwr. Ymgais prentis o fardd ydoedd i ganu clodydd i Owain Glyndŵr. Fodd bynnag, llwyddais i gipio'r wobr. Daeth y gynghanedd wedyn yn rhan annatod ohonof a diolchaf hyd heddiw am hyfforddiant sicr Euros Bowen yn hyn o beth.

Ond roedd dylanwad y prifardd a'r bardd arbrofol nodedig hwn yn fwy fyth arnaf a hynny am fod barddoniaeth Gymraeg yn rhywbeth mor fawr yn ei fywyd. Cofiaf yn ystod un wers iddo adrodd darnau helaeth o'r gerdd *Madog* inni. Gan droi ei gefn ar y dosbarth â'i ddwylo i fyny yn yr awyr, fe'n cipiwyd ar fwrdd y llong *Gwennan Gorn* ac ym mwrlwm afieithus y traethu gallem dyngu ein bod yn suddo gyda hi. Un o linellau anfarwol y gerdd arwrol hon yw: 'A bwlch ni ddangosodd lle bu.' Gosteg eithriadol wedyn yn yr ystafell. Yr oeddwn bellach yn sownd ym machyn y feirws. O'r adeg honno ymlaen, athro Cymraeg yr oeddwn am fod.

Gan fynd yn ôl am eiliad at yr awdl i Owain Glyndŵr, fe dynnodd y gerdd sylw gŵr arbennig iawn a fynnodd ei chyhoeddi ym misolyn y Bedyddwyr, sef *Seren Gomer*. Bron yn ddieithraid bob wythnos, byddai'n ymwelydd cyson ar yr aelwyd – cyfaill i'm tad yn y weinidogaeth a gweinidog Penuel, Capel y Bedyddwyr. Y gwron hwn oedd y Parch. Lewis Valentine – un o Gymry pwysicaf y ganrif ddiwethaf, arloeswr Plaid Cymru, ysgolhaig o'r radd flaenaf a llenor wrth reddf. Un o fanteision mwyaf bod yn fab i'r mans oedd cael y cyfle i gwrdd cymaint o weinidogion didwyll a deallus. Yn eu cwmni ffraeth clywem storïau diddorol a hanesion di-rifedi hynt a helynt arwyr y ffydd yng Nghymru. (O Gymru, pa siâp fyddai arnat heddiw heb weinidogaeth y gwŷr cadarn hyn?) Fodd bynnag, yr oedd y seiadu wythnosol yng nghlyw y cawr yr oedd ei iaith goeth yn faeth digymar i unrhyw wrandawr. Caem hanesion y rhyfel, achos y Tân yn Llŷn, ei ddyddiau yn y carchar a'r dylanwadau eithriadol a fu arno. Arwr yn ei olwg oedd Emrys ap Iwan. Myfyriai yn wythnosol yn y clasuron Cymraeg. Gan ddechrau gyda Chanu Aneirin darllenai ac astudiai'n systematig yr holl weithiau llenyddol yn flynyddol. Dyfynnai ohonynt ac esboniai hwynt. Yn raddol daeth Llywarch Hen, Taliesin a Dafydd ap Gwilym yn rhan werthfawr o'm gwybod-aeth.

A minnau bellach yn y chweched dosbarth, y cwestiwn mawr oedd i ba goleg yr awn. Ni fu'n rhaid aros yn hir cyn cael yr ateb. Gwahoddwyd gŵr i ddarlithio ar y stori fer yn Ysgol y Grango. Hugh Bevan ydoedd hwn, darlithydd yn Adran y Gymraeg yng Ngholeg y Brifysgol yn Abertawe. Ar fy myw nid oeddwn wedi clywed y fath ddarlith erioed ac o'r funud honno penderfynais mai i Abertawe yr oeddwn am fynd.

A dyma fi'n ôl lle dechreuais. Mewn ystafell feddygol o bob man yn ystod fy nhymor cyntaf yn y Brifysgol, y sylweddolais beth oedd yr hunaniaeth Gymraeg a beth a olygai i fod yn Gymro o'r iawn ryw yn hanner olaf yr ugeinfed ganrif. Fel gelen glynodd y label 'very Welsh' gyda fi trwy'r holl flynyddoedd. Naddo ches i ddim gwared â'r haint hwn ac ni cheisiais gelu fy acen o gwbl. Ar ôl treulio blynyddoedd yn addysgu Cymraeg a Chymraeg Ail Iaith yn siroedd y De, bod yn Hyfforddwr Cenedlaethol y Gymraeg yn sgîl dyfodiad y Cwricwlwm Cenedlaethol, ac yna yn ymgynghorydd ac arolygwr addysg, ymfalchïaf mai bywhau a gwydnhau wnaeth y feirws. Pe bai Dr. Dan, yr arbenigwr ar aspirin, yn fy ailarchwilio heddiw diau mai ei ddyfarniad fyddai: 'No change: very, very Welsh.'

Beth yw'r Ots?

gan

DYLAN IORWERTH

Cymru yw . . .
Sefyll ar y dibyn ymyl twll chwarel a chlywed y llechi'n symud, gan wneud sŵn fel llestri'n torri. Yn y gwaelod, mae'r dŵr anniddig. Uwchben, mae'r gwynt yn griddfan. Yn fa'ma yr aeth Bennet Williams i'r dyfnder ola', du.

Cymru yw . . .
Peidio â throi yng Nghaerdydd wrth glywed gair o Gymraeg, ond gwneud hynny yn Aberteifi.

Cymru yw . . .
Ymddiried mewn pechadur sy'n siarad iaith y nefoedd, a chael fy nhwyllo eto.

Cymru yw . . .
Mwytho'r mwsog ar goeden. Clywed oglau'r rhisgl. Teimlo'r pydredd yn mallu dan fy nwylo. Bywyd yn mynd yn ei flaen.

Cymru yw . . .
Gweld fflam o goch yn llamu'n sydyn yn y canghennau, a dychmygu mai gwiwer oedd yno.

Cymru yw . . .
Cicio sodlau mewn ciosg bws a'r nodwyddau'n tasgu o dan draed. Graffiti yn lle cynghanedd. Y Fam Gymreig yn gwthio un a thynnu'r llall gan chwilio am eu tadau.

Cymru yw . . .
Cân werin yn torri trwy fwg sigaréts a sobreiddio'r bois wrth y bar.

Cymru yw . . .
Meic Stevens yn tiwnio'i gitâr.

Cymru yw . . .
Morwyn y fro yn cario'r blodau, a breuddwydio am gariad neith-
iwr. Cerrig plastig yr Orsedd yn cael eu chwythu gan y gwynt. "A
oes heddwch?" . . . ac awyren Hawk yn mynd heibio.

Cymru yw . . .
Cynulliad. Adeilad coch ym Mae Caerdydd, heb ddim ond ychydig
o wydr. Y tu allan, twll . . . a'r gwleidyddion eisiau bod ynddo.

Cymru yw . . .
Sefyll wrth y pympiau cwrw a'r barman yn edrych trwydda' i.

Cymru yw . . .
Map heb linellau cochion y mesurwyr tir na ffiniau'r pwyllgorydd-
ion. Map gyda dim ond enwau. Enwau, yn treiddio i'r tir fel dŵr y
mynydd, yn codi i'r awyr fel mwg mawn o simnai, neu gawod o
wreichion ffwrnais. Enwau'n adrodd straeon a chwedlau, yn adlais
o chwerthin a churiad morthwylion, yn acennu tro'r tymhorau, yn
sibrwd defosiwn y saint. Cyn i'r llinellau ddod i'w carcharu.

Cymru yw . . .
Gaeaf cynnes, heb rew i chwalu'r pridd. Blodau mis Mawrth ym
mis Chwefror a ieir bach yr haf yn drwsgl.

Cymru yw . . .
Peint pnawn a malu awyr. Munud o ddistawrwydd mewn capel a'r
ffenest liw yn creu enfys ar y muriau.

Cymru yw . . .
Coler am wddw gweinidog, fel darn o offer S + M rhagluniaeth.

Cymru yw . . .
Caernarfon ar nos Sadwrn. Cwffio. Caru. Chwydu. Fandaliaeth.
Chwerthin. Dawnsio. Lyshio. Y lle mwya' Cymraeg yn y byd.

Cymru yw . . .
Siom. Sylweddoli'n sydyn fod iaith Beca yn iaith Maggie. Ein
hogia' ni oedd yn ennill Oscar yn Rorke's Drift a gwneud ffortiwn
yn Awstralia. Cas i neb?

Cymru yw . . .
Un bwthyn bach, a wal y plas yn mynd rownd-ddo.

Cymru yw . . .
Chwibaniad coll, hiraethus, y gylfinir a'r atgof ohoni hi'n codi
uwchben y corsydd agored, lle mae'r coed pin. Ymhobman, mae
yna dyllau yn yr awyr lle mae'r adar wedi mynd.

Cymru yw . . .
Trio pasio Mansel Davies Llanfyrnach . . . gerllaw Corris . . . yn y
niwl.

Cymru yw . . .
Cynhyrfu'n lân wrth wylio'r crysau coch. Gwirioni wrth weld gwib,
a'r bêl yn troelli fel gobeithion rhwng y pyst. Dechrau dathlu, gan
wybod y byddwn ni'n colli.

Cymru yw . . .
Hymns and arias . . . a neb yn cofio'r geiriau.

Cymru yw . . .
Brymi mewn tafarn a'i lais fel rhygnu'r ceir tros filltiroedd maith
Pumlumon. Byddin dan bwysau eu shellsuits, yn chwifio manylion
y gwerthwyr tai fel gwaywffyn yn eu dwylo.

Cymru yw . . .
"Ydach chi'n siarad Cymraeg?"

"You what?"
"Ydach chi'n siarad Cymraeg?"
"Speak English."
"Iawn, OK then, sorry."

Cymru yw . . .
Gorfoledd. Cerdded i mewn i lond lle o siaradwyr Cymraeg a nabod neb.

Cymru yw . . .
Gwirioni ar lwyddiant siaradwyr Cymraeg. Hollywood, San Steffan a'r Brits, dyma ni ar ein ffordd . . . i ddangos ein bod ni'n gallu ei gwneud hi. Ond term Saesneg yw Cool Cymru.

Cymru yw . . .
Ngs tstn n Gmrg.

Cymru yw . . .
Cyrff chwyslyd ym Maes B . . . a finnau'n rhy foel i fentro.

Cymru yw . . .
Caru methu mentro.

Cymry yw . . .
Ni . . . a nhwthau hefyd.

Bryan Davies (Ferndale).

Brian Davies (Pontypridd).

Brian Davies (Ystradgynlais).

Euros Jones Evans.

Dylan Iorwerth.

Leon.

Karen Owen.

J. Beynon Phillips.

Clive Rowlands.

Annete Thomas.

Marjorie Showalla.

Maggie Wagstaff.

Phyllis Wagstaff.

Roger Whatcott.

Iwan Bryn Williams.

Jean E. Williams.

Y Golygydd/The Editor

T. Graham Williams ('Cefnfab').

Diolchiadau/Acknowledgements

Hoffwn gydnabod cymorth y canlynol am yr amser a'u hymdrech tuag at gynhyrchu y llyfr hwn.

I wish to acknowledge the following for their time and effort in helping towards producing this book:

Lynnford Jones, Val Whatcott, Lorraine Scourfield, Jeff Townes, Phillip Green, Richard Wagstaff, Mike Edmunds, W. J. Evans, Hywel Bowen, Mansel Jones, Pat Jones Evans, Emyr Wyn Jones, Ysgol Gynradd Gymraeg Draddodiadol Rhiwfawr, Menter Gwrhyd, Emyr Williams, Guto Rhys Huws, Jan Poole, Ian Waterhouse, Jessica Jones, Monica Mahoney a hefyd llawer mwy na enwir yma. Eu cyngor a'u hanogaeth gyson a wnaeth y cyfan oll yn bosib./There are also several others who are not mentioned here, but whose advice and constant encouragement made it all possible.

Llyfryddiaeth/Bibliography

Cefnfab, nodiadau o'r ddarlith *'Byd dirgel Dylan Thomas'.*/Notes taken from Cefnfab's lecture *'The undiscovered world of Dylan Thomas'*.

Crossley-Holland, P., Article on John Parry – Groves Dictionary of Music, 5th edition (1954).

Edwards, O. T., A Fourteenth Century Welsh Sarum Antiphonal (NLWMS20 54), 1987.

Ferris, Paul, *Dylan Thomas: The Biography* (J. M. Dent, 1977).

Martin, Nansi, *'Gwilym Marles'* (Gwasg Gomer Press, 1979).

Rousseau: *Dictionnaire de musique 1767.*

Williams, Professor David, Aberystwyth University, *'The Rebecca Riots'*.

Ynyscedwyn Estate Papers, Ystradgynlais – Swansea Archives.

Nodiadau

Ymddangosodd y gerdd 'Rhwydi' gan Iwan Bryn Williams gyntaf yn *Llên y Llannau*, 1998, yn ogystal â rhan o'r gerdd 'Amgueddfa Werin Cymru' gan Cefnfab yn y flwyddyn 2000.

Notes

(These notes are in relation to both pages 23 and 31)

Gwilym Marles was Dylan Thomas' great uncle. He was baptised William Thomas, but in later years adopted the bardic pen name of 'Gwilym Marles'. ('Marlais', taken from the colloquial word 'Marles', was Thomas' second name.) Gwilym was a minister at a Unitarian chapel in Llwynrhydowen, whilst he also founded the Llandysul Grammar School. Gwilym was held in high esteem in Cardiganshire, through the considerate manner in which he cared for the well being of the people. This was manifested when between three and four thousand gathered at an open air service outside the chapel, during the first Sunday after he and the congregation had been turned out of the premises. (It is interesting to note that this large number of people had congregated there when it was only decided to do so a few hours earlier. This incident was similar to the manner in which people of the same area – and at about the same period of time – had collected together at Llandysul station in a spontaneous gesture of support to the Ffynnonllywelyn family. Even more remarkable is that all this took place before the technology of modern communication.) It should be mentioned that not only was Gwilym Marles a highly respected minister but also a fine hymn writer. These hymns – although written in Welsh – have the same undertone and symbolic representation to Dylan Thomas' own work, confirming the contributing influence of his family's background.